Welcome to Wine

AN ILLUSTRATED GUIDE
TO ALL YOU *REALLY* NEED TO KNOW

Written and Illustrated by
MADELYNE MEYER

TRANSLATED BY RACHEL WARD

THE EXPERIMENT

NEW YORK

CONTENTS

The Basics

Tasting

MY WAY INTO WINE

FROM CROWBARS TO CORKSCREWS

I drink wine. I love wine. I have no clue about wine.

This is how my journey from wine amateur to wine expert got started—and the beginning of my story:

Growing up in a Swiss family in the wine trade, I spent my school vacations in wine cellars—wielding crowbars to open wooden crates, putting bottles on conveyor belts, slapping on custom labels, and filling bag-in-box cartons with cooking wine. I loved those jobs. And I particularly loved the smell of wine being bottled, and the cheery men in overalls, buzzing about on their pallet trucks, assembling the wine for our customers.

A few years later, wine became the subject of my bachelor's thesis, which dealt with the process of recognizing international wine trends. I traveled with our CEO to Europe's biggest wine trade fair, ProWein in Düsseldorf, Germany. While there, we met wine producers who saw their job as a passion and a calling. I caught the wine bug on the spot and knew that I would never want to work in any other profession. I completed assorted wine courses and got the chance to work at two California wineries as a hospitality intern. It was there that I also met my incredibly dynamic mentor, Lindsey, and, in the end, I really have her to thank for my career in the wine world. She presented me with new challenges on a weekly basis, pushed me to become a Certified Specialist of Wine, and constantly put me to the test. She was my greatest inspiration.

On the way toward this qualification, I very quickly realized that drinking wine is a lot more fun than learning about wine. The course material reminded me of an algebra lesson: rational, technical, and dry. What had happened to the joy—the passion? And how on earth was I going to remember all this information with a brain like a goldfish and the concentration span of a puppy?

Well, thanks to an educational therapist I had in my teens, I learned I was no goldfish after all. I was taught to use colors and shapes to learn maps, words, and formulas by heart, and in the process I realized that I have a very visual mind—that's all! I was able to earn my bachelor's degree in business by sketching thousands upon thousands of multicolored, outsize mind-maps. And I couldn't shake the thought that there might be plenty of people out there who are just like me.

So I began sketching everything I'd learned about wine through illustrations. And I started thinking about creating a blog to share this knowledge in a fun and informative way.

When I led tastings at the wineries in California, I noticed that so many people—from the customers to the staff—were constantly talking about French wine, specifically Bordeaux. "They must be onto something," I thought. So I packed my bags and went to study wine marketing and management in Bordeaux, where I also had a job on the side as a marketing assistant to a wine merchant. I continued sketching and I started my blog— *Edvin*, "Educating Wine." Shortly thereafter I won a wine blogging competition in the "Wine and Travel" category. I felt I was onto something. So in the fall of 2016, once I'd finished my studies and my job in Bordeaux, I headed back home, now equipped with a bulging rucksack full of wine knowledge and a hefty dash of self-confidence.

When I returned, I looked around and realized that people needed wine explained to them in person in a way that easily made sense to them as much as illustrations made sense for me. So, I began to offer wine courses, which in turn sparked plenty of fresh inspiration. Through these direct conversations with participants it became so clear to me what had been so unclear about the many facets of wine. Question after question I'd never considered myself came up and forced me to keep my explanations simple and to stay grounded—and my illustrations certainly helped, too. This led me to my particular style of wine education. And now these experiences and my blog have led to this book!

And that, dear reader, is all I want to share with you. This book makes understanding wine simple, with easy-to-understand drawings that make for as good a time as actually drinking wine . . . or at least comes close!

Now let's get to it. Cheers!

INTRODUCTION

MY MISSION:

Demystifying the language of wine

THE WINE WORLD SAYS:

"Such gorgeous toasted notes."

"Definitely far too young."

"Was there really only fifty percent malolactic fermentation?"

"Wow, I smell too much volatile acidity."

"The tannins need more time here to integrate and soften up."

"Yes, such a typically salty, mineral flavor."

"Amazingly astringent for a rosé."

I SAY:

"What the hell are they talking about?"

If your reaction is similar, you've come to the right place. This book is for the people—especially beginners—who are interested in wine but who don't want to deal with any of the pretension. I know what it's like! At the start of my career, I was just as overwhelmed. It wasn't just the course material—there were also lots of wine experts who completely discouraged me. Not to mention gawk-worthy wine racks that were intimidating to even approach. And then there were the wine lists, which make quite unreasonable demands of anyone who's ever learned to read. How many times have I sat in restaurants with a hundred-page wine list in my hands as the sommelier waited with a patient expression for my order? I'd be speechless: So many unpronounceable names!—and especially the French wines. I'd either stammer like a toddler or point silently with my shaky index finger at some random wine.

This is where my mission comes in: I know you've experienced scenarios like this, too, and I want to demystify the language of wine for you. We're in this together. I'll break it all down, categorize it, add colorful illustrations, and you'll never need to open a dictionary, Google, Wikipedia, or a wine atlas again. Easy peasy.

Your wine knowledge— pretension-free

The Basics

I am assuming that you're reading this book because you like wine. So, you're primarily interested in enjoying wine, but you've realized that you have no clue about it. That's exactly why this book exists: It simplifies everything related to wine for someone like you. The only precondition is that you can open a wine bottle (or get someone to do it for you!).

At this point, I should mention that I am not a sommelier and have no training in hotel management. Everything I know about hospitality I learned from Lindsey—my internship mentor who was an event manager.

It was an utterly unacademic way of learning, but entirely practical rather than theoretical. So, here, too, I've taken the liberty of breaking a few rules for one main purpose: practical applicability.

WINE GLASSES

One of the questions I get asked most often is whether the shape or type of a wine glass really has an effect, and whether you can genuinely taste a difference according to the glass. My answer is: Yes, and in a pretty big way! Try serving wine in a plastic cup. You'll find yourself booking an urgent appointment with your ear, nose, and throat doctor because the shape of the cup means you can't smell a thing.

There are dozens of shapes of wine glass, all designed to unlock the absolute maximum potential of a wine.

For starters, I recommend a universal glass, which shows off both white and red wines equally well.

But if you want to get down to fine details, I recommend the following:

Red wine glass with a rounded bowl and a narrower top (triangle shape)

For wines with elegant, fine aromas and a somewhat lighter body, such as pinot noir or gamay. Swirling the wine in the glass opens it up nicely, and the narrower opening means that the aromas don't escape right away.

Red wine glass with bowl and top of similar width (rectangular shape)

For wines with a more forceful aroma and a more powerful or heavier body, such as cabernet sauvignon or merlot. The generous cup allows the aromas to develop on contact with air while ascending up and out of the glass. The wider surface enables any possible scent of alcohol to escape.

Burgundy glass

Bordeaux glass

White wine glass with a slim cup and a narrower top

For practically any white wine, except heavy chardonnays, whose fuller body calls for a larger bowl. The tapering shape holds the floral aromas in the glass, and the acidity comes through nicely, enabling more aromas to unfold.

White wine glass for sparkling wine

Sparkling wines are fizzy, but they boast more than just carbon dioxide bubbles. Their aromas range from fruit to bakery-fresh bread. These scents can't develop in a narrow glass, known as flutes (or "test tubes" as I lovingly call them). We don't feel comfortable in a T-shirt that's too tight either. So I recommend using the same glass as for white wine.

Sparkling Wine Glass   White Wine Glass

Universal wine glass

A universal glass looks something like this. Ideal for white and red wines alike.

The difference between red and white wine glasses:

Red wines are generally more robust than whites, so their aromas and tasting notes are often better accentuated in a larger glass.

SERVING TEMPERATURE

At this point, I could go into the ideal serving temperature for every single variety of grape. I could do that, but I don't have to. Because, if we're honest, we only really pay attention to the correct serving temperature if we have company. On an average Netflix evening, you just grab the white wine out of the fridge or a bottle of red that's been sitting on the countertop for months.

That being said, your fridge should generally be set to a temperature of about 44°F (7°C).

White wine: 50–54°F (10–12°C)

Not chilled? Pop it in the freezer for twenty minutes or the fridge for an hour. The wine's in the fridge? Take it out fifteen minutes before pouring.

Rosé wine: 48–54°F (9–12°C)

Same as white wine.

Sparkling wine: 43–44°F (6–7°C)

Unchilled bubbly? Pop it in the freezer for an hour. Then place in the fridge until ready to serve.

Red wine: 57–64°F (14–18°C)

Too warm? Pop it in the freezer for fifteen minutes or the fridge for half an hour. Serve within ten to fifteen minutes.

Good to know

The warmer the wine, the better it can open up and show off its aromas. If the wine's too cold, the aroma molecules can end up so tightly packed that you can't even smell if it's corked. (A corked wine is one that smells of mold and must.)

43–44°F (6–7°C)

48–54°F (9–12°C)

57–64°F (14–18°C)

HANDLING BOTTLES AND GLASSES

CUT AWAY THE CAP AT THE BOTTOM EDGE AND REMOVE IT.

To keep the wine from flowing over the foil. Prevents drips.

AS YOU POUR, TURN THE BOTTLE 180 DEGREES CLOCKWISE.

Don't rest the bottle on the rim of the glass.

1 INCH
(2.5 CM)

HOLD THE BOTTLE IN THE MIDDLE.

Pour 5 ounces (150 ml), which is about ⅓ of a glass.

⅓

THE GLASS HAS A STEM FOR A REASON.

Hold the glass by the stem, not the bowl.
Otherwise, the wine will get warm.

SHELF LIFE

Apparently, there are admirable people who don't always finish a bottle of wine in one sitting. I don't quite understand it myself . . . nevertheless this section is for all those virtuous, disciplined wine lovers.

Ground rules for good storage:

White wines

- Close with the original top.
- Pop it in the fridge.
- Keep it upright.

Red wines

- Close with the original closure or a wine stopper. Keep it in a dark place away from sunlight or in the fridge.
- Keep it upright.

Sparkling wines

Always use a specialized sparkling wine stopper!

To withstand the high pressure from the carbon dioxide, these stoppers have a larger diameter and thus also a larger capacity than the ones for still wines. They're also secured with a clamp.

- Pop it in the fridge.
- Keep it upright. Don't lay it down.

By the way: Does the trick about sticking the handle of a teaspoon in an open bottle of sparkling wine keep the fizz alive? Nope. You might just as well place a fork on a slice of bread to keep it from drying out.

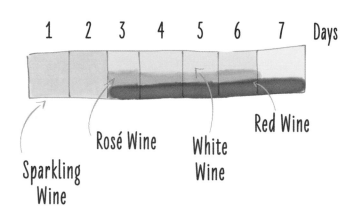

1 2 3 4 5 6 7 Days

Sparkling Wine

Rosé Wine

White Wine

Red Wine

Good to know

An opened bottle of wine will generally keep for about three days. But there are always exceptions.

TO DECANT

Decanting wine is probably the simplest way to impress your guests. It can only be topped by sabering (opening a champagne bottle by slicing off the cork with a sword).

Imagine: The wine you want to serve has been lying in the bottle for at least a year, completely protected from incoming oxygen. And now imagine having to survive a year without oxygen yourself.

Stressful, huh?

The bottom line is: Every wine, even a young one—whether white or red—likes a gulp of oxygen once it's been opened, so that it can breathe and expand.

When you decant a wine, sediment should stay in the shoulder of the bottle. Only the pure wine goes into the decanter. If any residue does still make it into the decanter, it gets caught here when you pour it into the glass.

DECANTING OLDER, MATURE WINES
Separating sediment/deposits (phenolic compounds) from the wine

You have to be more careful with older, more mature wines. If the wine comes into contact with too much oxygen, it can oxidize quickly (turn to vinegar).

There's no need to worry about choosing a perfect decanter: a glass jug, a flower vase, or any other glass container from around the house will do.

Basically, younger wines should be decanted into a decanter with a rounder belly (more contact with the oxygen), older wines into a slimmer decanter (less contact with the oxygen). When decanting older wines, it's all about separating the sediment from the wine: Sediment should remain in the bottle and only the pure wine should end up in the decanter. So, let all the sediment settle on the bottom before pouring the wine into the decanter.

DECANTING YOUNG WINES
Aerating/allowing the wine to breathe

Oxygen enables the aromas to develop properly.

So it's good for young wines, which tend to be closed/tight.

In here, the wine gets plenty of air.

You can also decant wine into a vase, a glass jug, or even Cinderella's glass slipper.

CLOSURES AND BOTTLE SHAPES

CLOSURES

For those from the "Old World" of wine (Northern Europe and the Mediterranean, the Middle East, and North Africa) bottle closures are a hot topic, fervently debated and much discussed, while in the "New World" of wine (the Americas, South Africa, Australia, and New Zealand) not a soul is interested in it. This predominantly comes down to tradition.

Wine has been produced in the "Old World" for over seven thousand years. Wine corks, as we know them today, were first used in the late eighteenth century, although their origins date back to ancient Greece. Even then, simple cork bungs were used to seal bottles. Wine has only been produced in the "New World" since the mid-sixteenth century, so tradition ranks a bit lower.

So which form of closure is better? New studies are being published all the time, taking turns to prove the advantages and disadvantages of screw caps or corks.

The following four points are worth considering:

1. We love the romantic pop of a cork when we open a bottle.

2. On the other hand, we also appreciate how easy it is to open a screw cap. And being relieved of the pressure to determine possible cork taint is a perk! (A screw cap wine can still smell corked, though [see p. 32].)

Good to know

Unopened wine with a cork should be stored horizontally. The cork will remain airtight so long as the wine keeps it moist. If the bottle is stored upright, the cork will dry out, become porous, and let in too much oxygen, and the wine will turn into vinegar.

Sparkling wine

3. Around 99 percent of wines on the market today can be enjoyed immediately, or within a year. This makes the closure irrelevant.

4. The remaining 1 percent of wines, with the potential to be stored for between five and fifty years, needs slow and steady minimal air supply to fully develop. This is ensured by the oxygen in the cork and the oxygen dissolved in the wine. These days, there are also screw caps that are specifically produced to allow exactly this steady yet minimal ingress of air. Only time will tell if bottle-aging over fifty years with a screw cap can match that of a cork.

BOTTLES

This is pretty dry stuff, about as inspiring as an instruction manual on building furniture. But the question keeps coming up, so here are a few notes on the three most common types of bottle.

1. Alsace (Flute)

In the past, wines from Alsace were transported along the Rhine on small barges. Its long, slim shape allowed more bottles to be loaded and transported.

Alsace shape

2. Burgundy

The Burgundy style is the oldest bottle shape. It is the easiest shape for a glass blower to form.

3. Bordeaux

Red Bordeaux wines are assemblages (blends of two or more grape varieties) made of cabernet sauvignon, cabernet franc, merlot, petit verdot, and malbec: grapes with thicker skins, which produce powerful tannins. The bottle's broad shoulders help catch the sediment when these mature wines are decanted. Mind you, this requires a certain degree of talent in pouring.

Burgundy shape

Bordeaux shape

FOOD AND WINE PAIRING

Now we're coming to the best part of the book: eating and drinking. I'm sure you agree with me that there's nothing better than enjoying a good meal together with a good wine. As my own cooking experience begins (and ends) with fish sticks, I'm utterly fascinated by the talent of creative cooks. Finding the right wine to match their works of art on the plate is sheer joy.

There are countless rules for correct food and wine pairings, which all make perfect sense but collectively can be rather overwhelming. So we'll focus our attention on the key reference points and round them off with a few concrete suggestions.

THE MEAL AS A STARTING POINT

- White meat—white wine   Red meat—red wine
- Light sauce—lighter wine   Heavy sauce—heavier wine
- Intensely flavorful dishes—intensely flavorful wines
- Spicy dishes—sweet white wines with low alcohol, or otherwise your whole mouth will be on fire
- Fatty dishes—full-bodied red wines with firm tannins (more to come on tannins on page 38)
- Chocolate—port or Madeira. The wine needs to be sweeter than the chocolate or your mouth will dry out.

THE WINE AS A STARTING POINT

- Wines with high acidity need foods with acidity (or the meal will taste bland).
- Wines with residual sweetness need sweetness in the food (or the food will taste bitter).
- Salt in food intensifies the taste of the wine.
- Food and wine from the same region belong together like Jay-Z and Beyoncé.

FOOD AND WINE PAIRING

FAVORITE FOODS

To make it easier for you to put into practice, here are a few very simple, crystal-clear suggestions for food and wine pairings.

Cheese ravioli: milder, rounder white wine, such as chardonnay

White meat: aromatic, refreshing wine, such as viognier

Sushi: more powerful, punchier white wine, such as riesling *kabinett* with slight residual sweetness

Red meat: heftier, more powerful red wine, such as malbec, syrah (or shiraz), or a Bordeaux

Veal scallopini: milder, rounder white wine, such as grüner veltliner

Spaghetti, pizza: rounder, softer red wine, such as merlot

Sausage: beer—let's not kid ourselves!

Fish, fried or grilled: milder, rounder white wine, such as pinot blanc

Shellfish: crisper, fresher white wine, such as Muscadet

Fish, poached: crisper, fresher white wine, such as sauvignon blanc

Vegetarian dishes: milder, rounder white wine, such as garnacha blanca

Mexican cuisine: lighter, austere red wine, such as Chianti

Asian cuisine: lusher, fuller white wine, such as moscato d'Asti, or riesling with a slight residual sweetness

But don't forget: Rules are made to be broken—as long as no one gets sick!

CHEESE

My absolute favorite cheese-and-wine pairing is fondue and pinot noir. In the wintertime, I don't go a single week without this all-around comforting combination.

For everyone else who doesn't enjoy melted cheese with wine every week, here are the most elementary pairings.

Hard cheese: red wine like merlot or pinot noir

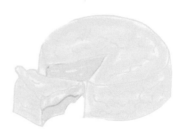

Soft cheese: any sparkling wine

Goat cheese: white wine like sauvignon blanc or riesling

Blue cheese: dessert wine like Sauternes, port, ice wine, or *Trockenbeerenauslese* (now *there's* a mouthful; more on that wine on page 37)

WHICH WINE FOR WHICH OCCASION

Wine connects people like practically nothing else. After all, a bottle of wine is usually shared. (Pro tip: Make sure you always make eye contact when you say "cheers" and clink glasses—it builds a strong connection between you and your guest!) Choosing the right wine for the right occasion, or as a gift, sometimes takes a little courage when we know our wine knowledge is being put to the test for all to see. But here's one less thing to worry about: Most people don't actually know that much about wine—they just pretend that they do.

So: Which wine for which occasion, and how do you figure out how much you need?

Here come the answers.

Aperitif (predinner)

A sauvignon blanc, for example, would be appropriate. Crisp and fresh, it revives your spirits after a long day at work.

A present for your boss, dinner with the in-laws, or any other event that makes you sweat

Never bring a Bordeaux or Burgundy (they only lead to questions that you can't answer and, probably, embarrassment). The best way to play it safe is to give them a brunello di Montalcino.

This is a prestigious wine, which is always made of 100 percent sangiovese grapes and so is super-easy to explain.

Gift
Brunello di Montalcino

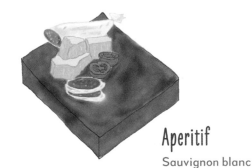

Aperitif
Sauvignon blanc

Celebrations
Cava (Spanish
sparkling wine)

Celebrating a new stage in life

When celebrating a new house, a wedding, a promotion, or any other occasion that marks a new direction in your life, cava, a Spanish sparkling wine, is ideal.

It should be dry, not sweet. Because cava is made the same way as Champagne but costs less, it's also not as painful if any of the aforementioned undertakings don't work out.

Date

I'd recommend a Valpolicella ripasso or an amarone, because the higher alcohol content immediately relaxes you . . .

Date
Valpolicella ripasso,
amarone

Family gatherings
Tempranillo

Family gathering

A tempranillo is fruity, not particularly heavy, and a crowd-pleaser. At least you can be sure the wine won't start any fights.

For taking to a party

Wine or sparkling wine from the local area or the closest wine region makes for a personal touch and gives you something to talk about.

Party
A wine from the local region

CALCULATING QUANTITIES

Aperitif
- Wine: One glass (150 ml) per person, per hour
- For a one-hour happy hour: One 750 ml bottle for five people (reserve: two bottles)
- Water: One glass (150 ml) per person, per hour

Magic formula to ward off hangovers: Always drink equal quantities of water and wine.

Dinner
The following quantities will see you through an entire evening:
- Wine for bibulous nondrivers: Five to six glasses (one 750 ml bottle) per person
- Wine for nondrivers who have to get up at 6:00 the next morning: Two to three glasses (350 ml) per person
- Water: Six to seven glasses (1 L) per person

150 ML (5 FL. OZ.)

WINE GLASS VOLUME
Restaurants generally serve between 100 to 200 ml per glass. For you or your guests, I'd recommend 150 ml.

REMOVING WINE STAINS

Fresh stains are much easier
to deal with than dried ones, so
always act quickly.

MY TIPS

Carbonated mineral water

1. Immediately dab the outside of
   the stain dry with a white cloth;
   don't rub it.
2. Dab the stain clean with plenty
   of carbonated water (the more
   carbon dioxide the better).
3. Let it air-dry.
4. Pop it in the washing machine.

Salt

1. Pour a small heap of salt on the
   stain, going over the edges. The
   salt will draw the moisture up
   out of the fabric.
2. Let the salt dry into the stain.
3. Remove the salt.
4. Pop it in the washing machine.

**Glass cleaner for
dried-in stains**

1. Spray the stain with colorless
   glass cleaner.
2. Scrub thoroughly.
3. Allow to dry.
4. Pop it in the washing machine.

WINES FOR CELLARING

About 99 percent of the wines you find on the shelves in your wine shop are ready to drink right away or within a year.

If you buy one of the wines listed on the following page, you'd be well advised to pay attention to the year. These wines need, roughly speaking, at least five years to develop their full potential. These wines boast intense tannins and a good acidity. They often have 13 percent alcohol by volume (or more) and are known for their powerful body. I like to call them the B-wines because of their shared initial.

A WINE CELLAR FOR THE HARD CORE

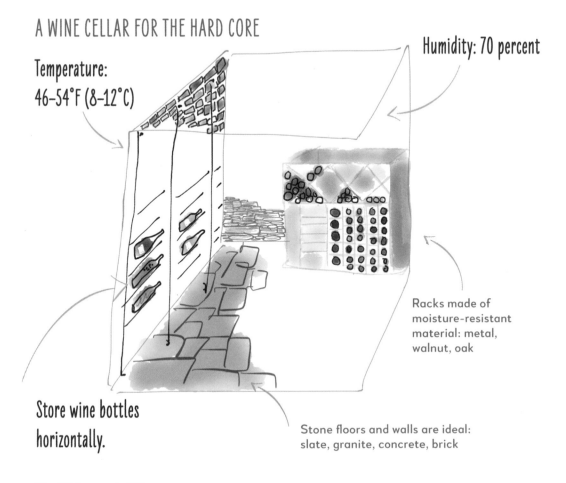

Temperature: 46–54°F (8–12°C)

Humidity: 70 percent

Racks made of moisture-resistant material: metal, walnut, oak

Store wine bottles horizontally.

Stone floors and walls are ideal: slate, granite, concrete, brick

- *Barolo:* 15+ years
- *Barbaresco:* 15+ years
- *Bordeaux:* 20+ years
- *Brunello:* 15+ years
- *Burgundy:* 12+ years
- Wines from *Rioja* and *Ribera del Duero* (both 20 years or more) and the *Napa Valley* (12 years or more) also have great aging potential. (It's just a shame these regions don't begin with B.)

It is important to note here that only the premium wines from the best years by top producers with outstanding terroir have the hidden talents that enable their wines to be cellared for decades. Over time, the tannins and the acidity integrate into the wine. The wines end up altogether rounder and silkier, and also develop complex, earthy, spicy, and sometimes animal notes.

White wines can also be cellared: Mature whites gain in complexity. Chardonnay, for example, develops nutty aromas, while rieslings take on delicate gasoline-like notes (in a good way):

- *Chardonnay* from Burgundy
- *Grüner veltliner* with good acidity and residual sugar
- *Rieslings* with a pronounced acidity (especially the sweeter rieslings)
- *Dessert wines:* The residual sugar preserves the wine from oxidation.

Good to know

For investors: Not every wine that is suitable for cellaring will increase in value with the years. The vintage makes all the difference. Ask a specialist for advice.

If you don't have a wine cellar, a dark, cool place will work, too.

Avoid light, heat, and major fluctuations in temperature.

DEALING WITH HANGOVERS

You cautiously open your eyes. All of a sudden, the daylight stabs them like arrowheads from hell. Your head is buzzing and your mouth feels like a sandstorm has swept through it. It's an open-and-shut case: You've been overdoing it again. Good morning, hangover!

Blame for the hangover lies not with the alcohol, but with the drinker. The fact of the matter is there are some people who are more sensitive to alcohol, while others seem to be bottomless barrels. It's also possible that some people react more strongly to certain constituents of wine, such as the natural protein histamine (which is found particularly in red wine).

What is the actual effect of excessive alcohol consumption on your body? It deprives the body of water. The parched liver tries to get ahold of moisture from elsewhere in the body, wherever it possibly can—and especially the brain. This ultimately leads to the pounding headache.

So, here's the remedy:

- Gallons of water
- Minerals
  - Calcium: good for the digestion
  - Magnesium: fights fatigue
  - Vitamins: help get your mind back on its feet
  - Zinc: boosts cognitive processes and helps with clear thinking
- Vegetable stock: restores your mineral levels
- Hot water with fresh ginger and lemon: cranks up your metabolism and detoxes

By the way: The much-vaunted "hair of the dog" (another alcoholic drink to "cure" your hangover) and fatty foods only boost your mood—they don't help your body.

Enough babbling,
it's time for a
tasting!

Tasting

"**J**ust last week, I had a red wine. It was amazing! No idea why I liked it so much, but it was great." Does this kind of remark sound familiar to you? Do you know which wines you currently like and which you don't? Is that about the limit of your wine skills?

I can assure you, you're not alone.

In this chapter, you'll learn why you prefer certain wines or why you just like everything.

A little tip to get started: Whether you're at home or in a restaurant, while enjoying those first few sips of wine, take a minute or two to focus on what's in your glass. Focus. Taste. Remember. This will help you find your own wine style.

THE EYE

As soon as the wine is in the glass, it's showing you what to do next (apart from drinking up). Tilting the glass toward a white surface is the best way to see what's going on in there. If you hold your glass up in the air and peer in from underneath, the only thing you'll reveal is your own cluelessness. What's to see up there?

It's impossible to judge the quality of a wine by appearance alone. Just like with people.

Good to know

The longer the white grape juice (the pulp) comes into contact with the grape skins, the more color it will take on—similar to how water gets darker the longer you leave a teabag in a mug. But a pale color doesn't necessarily mean a lighter wine with low alcohol. Don't be deceived! Wines can be sneaky.

- Does the wine shine like your windows after a spring cleaning? Perfect, drink on.

- Is there sediment swimming in the wine? Don't panic, it won't do you or the wine any harm, but it might be a good idea to decant it (see page 8).

- Are there small crystals settling on the bottom of the glass? Those are tartrates (potassium bitartrate). This occurs, for example, when minerals combine with acid at low storage temperatures. Tartrates have no effect on the taste of the wine.

- Does the wine look slightly opaque? This might be intentional. The winemaker might have decided against filtering the wine so as to take nothing away from it. The clouding has no impact on the quality.

Many so-called wine connoisseurs insist that the wine legs (or "wine tears" or "church windows") that appear when you swirl the glass are a sign of quality. Humbug! This phenomenon is caused by alcohol evaporating as the glass is swirled, and/or from high residual sugar in the wine.

A LOT OF LEG

Skinny legs

Alcohol +

Legs (or pointed church windows) that flow down and close together mean a lot of alcohol. If the label gives a lower alcohol percentage, you can assume that the wine has a greater residual sweetness (more sugar). The legs look viscous (gooey) like honey or syrup.

Fuller legs

Alcohol −

Legs that flow down further apart (or more rounded, wider church windows) mean less alcohol, more sugar.

Lower alcohol volumes: 5–10%
Moderate alcohol volumes: 11–14%
Higher alcohol volumes: 15–16%

Even 0.5% more or less alcohol makes a major and noticeable difference.

THE NOSE

DISCOVERING SCENTS

Aroma and effect:

Restrained

You can't smell a thing.

Present

You can smell something.

Insistent (expressive)

You can smell a whole, jam-packed botanical garden.

Floral

More common in white wines

Earthy

More common in red wines

Herbal

Fruity

Secondary aromas

From oak barrels, aging, and malolactic fermentation

Spicy

The smell of the wine as perceived in the nose makes a major contribution to the overall impression. There are people with more sensitive noses, and others who perceive the aromas better on their palate. It all depends on the person. That being said, the nose is particularly important in the tasting process for detecting wine flaws. But this isn't so easy for beginners. So, let's take a more in-depth look at the subject.

It's important to note that a wine often smells different from how it tastes. This is because the nose can only detect the aromas and possibly the alcohol. In red wine, the acidity, sweetness, and tannins also come out on the palate. They give the wine additional structure. As for smell, the aromas we can make out generally fall into the following categories: fruity, floral, herbal, spicy, earthy, and secondary aromas.

BLUFF AROMAS

If you're not quite sure what you can (or should) smell or taste, I recommend the following descriptions.

Nobody knows exactly what these aromas taste like in wine, but they'll get people nodding in agreement.

In red wine

Black currant leaves

In white wine

Gooseberries

Violets

Wood tar

WINE FLAWS

Recognizing flaws is one of the most difficult tasks in wine tasting. There are people whose sensitive noses simply pick up flaws instantly, and some who only notice a problem once half the bottle's been drunk. The ability to detect faults in a wine therefore depends on the following factors.

- Sensitive and well-developed olfactory nerves
- Experience
- Attention and concentration

Here are the most common defects that occur in white and red wines, and their characteristic smells.

	Cork taint	Oxidation	Volatile acidity	Sulfur (Böckser)
Smell	Mold Wet cardboard Damp cellars	Must, gasoline (reminiscent of sherry)	Acid, vinegar Flat Sour	Pungent odor Garlic Rotten eggs
Origin	The corked taste comes from a chemical substance with the impossible name of 2,4,6-trichloranisole (TCA), which develops in the cork bark, though cork taint can also be caused during wine production. The unpleasant-smelling TBA molecule (tribromoanisole) can come from any organic material (e.g., a wall) and doesn't necessarily have anything to do with the cork itself.	Excessive levels of oxygen in the bottle, whether before or after opening, can cause the wine to oxidize; this removes the fruity notes from the wine. The wine can also take on an orange-brown color, like a cut apple exposed to the air.	The fermentation process can give off acetic acid. Up to a point, this acid is an important carrier of flavor for the wine. If it oversteps the mark, however, the acid becomes very pungent and obtrusive.	Freshly bottled wines can have a sulfuric note, which should dissipate within a few minutes. It's worse when a wine seems to "fart" at you, though (Böckser). This off-note can be caused by sloppy work during production, excessive use of sulfur, or too little oxygenation.

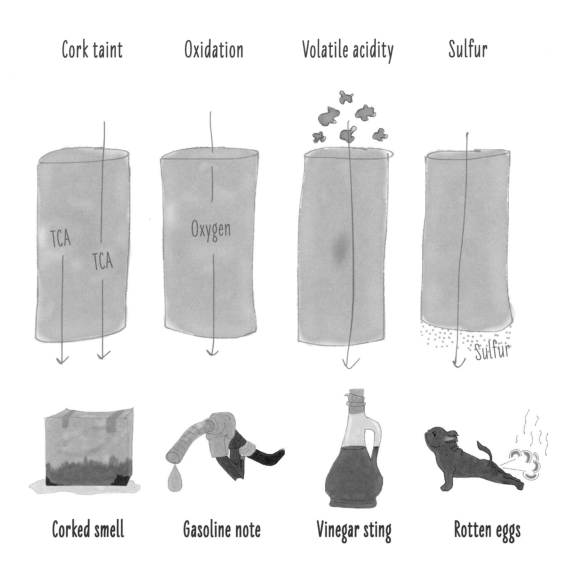

| Cork taint | Oxidation | Volatile acidity | Sulfur |
| Corked smell | Gasoline note | Vinegar sting | Rotten eggs |

Good to know
Don't sniff the cork to find out if there's a fault in the wine. Smell the wine—that's what you're drinking, not the cork.

THE PALATE

Hallelujah, we've made it! We've finally arrived at the sense of taste.

Let's get one thing out of the way first: I haven't got much time for elaborate flavor descriptions. I'm really not that interested in whether a riesling tastes more of apricot or peach. Nor can I see any reason to distinguish between the flavor of grapefruit juice and grapefruit peel. How does it benefit me or wine-loving buddies if I can smell hints of gooseberry in a sauvignon blanc? It won't get me a Nobel Prize, that's for sure. And I'm unlikely to get an appreciative pat on the shoulder from a rather irritated waiter either.

Honey face mask

AROMA PERCEPTIONS ARE EXTREMELY PERSONAL

Does this carmenère remind you of a chocolate bar? Fantastic.

You reckon that sangiovese smells like pesto? Fair enough then. You love moscato d'Asti, because it reminds you of your favorite honey face mask? That's totally up to you.

The complex, multifaceted nature of wine is all part of its enjoyment. The infinite number of aromas and tastes and varied structures means no two wines are the same.

And everybody can smell, taste, and even hear something different in their wine.

BODY

It's what's on the inside that counts...

The following elements give wine body.

Alcohol

You perceive alcohol as heat on the palate. If you start sweating, you're dealing with a very high-alcohol wine.

Good luck with it!

Tannins

Coarse tannins, which are mainly noticeable in red wines, leave you with a dry mouth, as if you'd been eating heaps of stale bread. It takes time for tannins to integrate into the wine.

Acidity

Acids get you salivating. So, if you start drooling, you're enjoying a wine with a rather pronounced acidity. If there's not enough acidity, the wine will taste flat.

Sugar

You notice sugar in wine much like Bailey's in coffee or honey in tea. This makes the wine a little fuller and heavier.

SUGAR STATS

Sugar barometer for still wines

Almost every wine has a little residual sweetness. Left to its own devices, the yeast would convert every gram of sugar into alcohol. This fermentation can be interrupted to keep a little sugar in the wine on purpose (residual sugar). This is done by the addition of sulfur and/or alcohol, by cooling, or by filtration—before the yeast has a chance to turn all the sugar into alcohol.

Residual sugar takes the form of fructose because glucose is converted into alcohol more quickly. The average wine has a residual sugar content of 4 grams per liter. But this is barely perceptible. Ordinary, mortal wine lovers don't tend to notice sugar in wine until about 25 g/L.

min. 45 g/L **Sweet**
e.g., riesling *Auslese*

12–45 g/L **Semisweet**
e.g., moscato d'Asti

MOST OF THE WINES WE
DRINK CAN BE FOUND HERE

4–12 g/L **Medium-dry**
e.g., gewürztraminer
(can also be produced in
a dry style)

0–4 g/L **Dry**
e.g., sauvignon blanc

SWEET WINES

Liquid gold

The following wines have a residual sugar level of at least 45 g/L and are thus considered sweet.

Sauternes, Barsac	Sweet white wines (sauvignon blanc, sémillon, muscadelle) from grapes affected by noble rot (botrytized grapes) in the Sauternes and Barsac region of Bordeaux, France.
Port	Fortified, sweet red wine from the Douro Valley, Portugal (originally from the harbor city of Porto). Typically sweet but it can also be produced dry.
Tokaji	Sweet white wine from grapes affected by noble rot in the Tokaj region, Hungary. Can also be produced dry.
Eiswein	Sweet white wines from frozen grapes in Austria and Germany. Also produced in New Zealand, Canada, and other regions.
Sherry labeled "Medium/ Cream/Pale Cream"	Fortified wine from Andalusia, Spain.
Riesling labeled "Spätlese/ Auslese/Beerenauslese/ Trockenbeerenauslese"	Sweet white wine made from overripe grapes and/or grapes affected by noble rot.

Spätlese: Sweet white wines from fully ripened grapes
Auslese: Sweet white wines from fully ripened, often botrytized and select grapes (the best and healthiest)
Beerenauslese: Sweet white wines from fully ripened, overripe, or botrytized grapes
Trockenbeerenauslese: Sweet white wines from 100 percent botrytized grapes

WINE STYLES OR CHARACTERS

As I've already said, my aim isn't for you to be able to detect dill and aniseed flavors in a wine once you've read this book (who wants those things in their wine anyway?!). It's way more important for you to learn to recognize different styles of wine—that is, the fundamental character of a wine.

Something like this: "Ah, gewürztraminer: powerful, punchy, possibly slightly sweet: perfect for my sushi marathon this evening."

Of course, there are countless types of wine styles, because every single wine has its own structure, and there are almost more exceptions than rules—which is precisely what tends to overwhelm people.

But we have to start somewhere, so I have taken the liberty of organizing white wines and red wines into four structural categories each. These eight structural pillars are intended as reminders and not as hard-and-fast rules.

The structure of white wine consists of three pillars: alcohol, acidity, and sugar.

The structure of red wine consists of four pillars: alcohol, acidity, sugar, and tannins. Tannins are found in grape skins and pips. A white wine can only contain tannins if the juice stays in longer contact with the skins, when it is then known as orange wine instead.

These pillars are like equalizers for music: the higher the pillar, the more intense the impact, and vice versa.

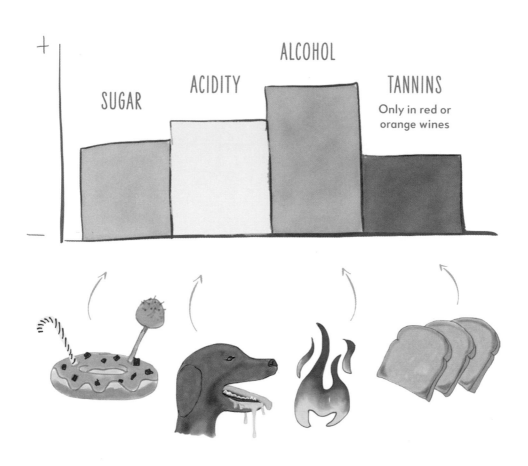

SUGAR   ACIDITY   ALCOHOL   TANNINS
Only in red or
orange wines

How we perceive and smell/taste these elements in wine

THE EIGHT STLYES OF WINE

WHITE WINE

MILD, ROUND
such as Chardonnay

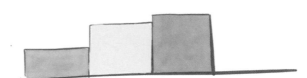

Very well balanced

CRISP, FRESH
such as sauvignon blanc

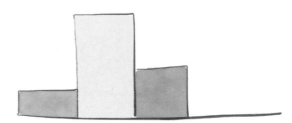

More noticeable acidity

POWERFUL, PUNCHY
such as gewürztraminer

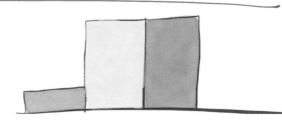

Pronounced acidity, very aromatic

LUSH, FULL
such as moscato d'Asti

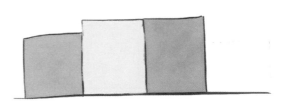

Noticeable residual sweetness

RED WINE

LIGHT, AUSTERE
such as pinot noir

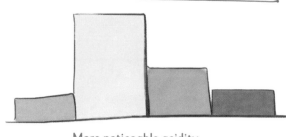

More noticeable acidity

ROUND, SOFT
such as merlot

Very well balanced

BOLD, RICH
such as cabernet sauvignon

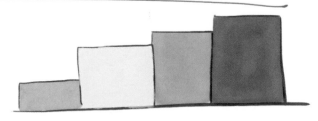

More powerful tannins

FULL-BODIED, OPULENT
such as amarone

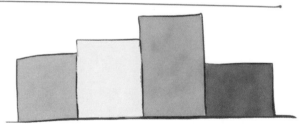

Full bodied, noticeable residual sweetness

THE AROMA CROSS

"Do you prefer fruity or dry wines?" Have you ever been asked this question? And did you know how to answer? Really. No big deal if you just stared back, dazed and confused. Because no matter how often this question is asked, it is always wrong! Dry and fruity aren't opposites. They're not mutually exclusive, because fruity wines can be dry, and vice versa.

This is why I created the aroma cross, which displays the oppositions in a very simple way.

Roughly speaking, they're as follows.

In relation to sugar

- Sweet versus dry wines

In relation to fruit

- Fruity versus mineral white wines
- Fruity versus earthy red wines

We can also add the following oppositions, but for the sake of simplicity, I've left them off the cross.

In relation to acidity

- Low versus pronounced acidity

In relation to tannins

- Softer tannins versus more robust tannins

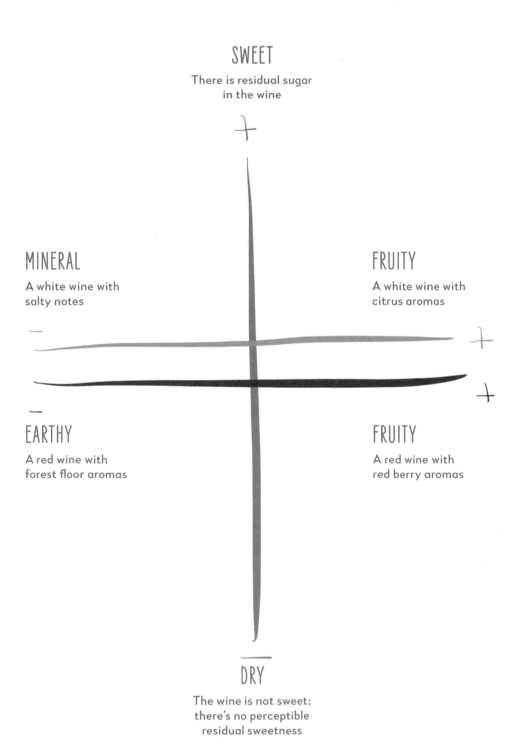

SWEET

There is residual sugar
in the wine

MINERAL

A white wine with
salty notes

FRUITY

A white wine with
citrus aromas

EARTHY

A red wine with
forest floor aromas

FRUITY

A red wine with
red berry aromas

DRY

The wine is not sweet;
there's no perceptible
residual sweetness

AROMA DEVELOPMENT

During my wine courses, I'm often asked where the flavors and aromas in wine come from. Questions like: "How is the licorice added to the petite syrah?" and "What animal does the leather in the nero d'Avola come from?"

A quick heads-up: The aromas in wine come from various biological and chemical reactions, with such unsexy names that they could instantly kill your love for wine. So, we'll leave the biology and chemistry lessons aside for now and concentrate on the essential factors.

1. PRIMARY AROMAS

You can't wander into a vineyard, pick a pinot blanc grape, bite into it, and expect the flavors of honeysuckle, orange blossom, and Pink Lady apples to flood your mouth. The grape contains the aroma potential—the precursor— but true aroma only comes through during wine production.

Here, we distinguish between the following basic aromas.

- Fruity: apple
- Floral: elderflower
- Spicy: licorice
- Herbal: basil
- Earthy: mushroom

From the specific grape variety

2. SECONDARY AROMAS

There's one thing everyone involved in wine can agree on: The quality of a wine depends on the work in the vineyard, not production or aging in the cellar. If the terroir (see page 60) is unsuitable—the soil is unhealthy, the vines too tightly planted and overloaded with grapes—and if they aren't pruned or harvested at the right time, you might as well kiss the work in the cellar goodbye.

Aromas from the vineyard

- From the terroir in and of itself (soil conditions, climate, altitude—more of this later on page 60).

The most important factor is the grape extract: The grape yield per vine is adjusted according to the age of the vine and the grape variety. The better these adjustments are made, and so long as the vines have enough access to groundwater, the richer the grape extract will be. The composition of these extracts will determine the color, the aroma, and above all the quality of the wine.

- **Climate conditions in any given year**
  In a warm/hot year, the sugar content of the grapes increases. This generally leads to ripe, lush wines. In a cool/cold year, the acidity remains relatively present and makes for much fresher wines. If the grape pips aren't able to mature properly, this has a particularly bad effect on the wine quality.

From cultivation and maturation

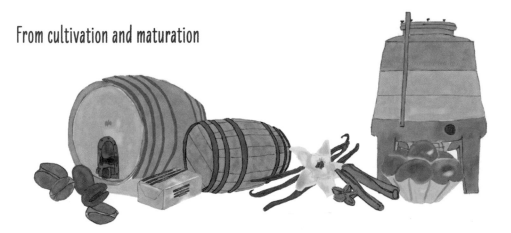

- There's no saving unripe grapes. They give a wine green, even woody flavors, like biting into an apple stem.

Aromas from vinification in the cellar

The winemaker's work can influence the aromas.

- **Fermentation**
  The winemaker determines the alcohol level (this gives the wine "body," i.e., richness) and how much sugar should remain in the wine. Yeasty flavors (croissants, butter, etc.) can also develop. Winemakers may also choose not to intervene at all, leaving the wine to ferment spontaneously (natural wine).

- **Maturation**
  Aging in a stainless steel tank lets a wine's fruity notes shine through, without influencing the wine. Through aging in wooden barrels, the wine can take on flavors from the wood (vanilla, cinnamon, chocolate, etc.).

The wooden barrel allows a minimal, slow ingress of oxygen that lets the wines become softer and silkier. Certain wines also take on a better flavor this way. Going a bit further, the inner walls of the barrel can even be toasted over fire. With this method, the wines develop such additional aromas as vanilla, cloves, butter, cinnamon, or coffee. (For more on barrel aging, see page 126.)

If the winemaker doesn't want the influence of wood, but the wine still needs to breathe, it can also be aged in a concrete egg or amphora. This allows a minimal amount of oxygen into the wine. When it comes to the influence of oxygen, the effects of a concrete egg lie somewhere between a steel tank and a wooden barrel.

Good to know

Vintage = the year the grapes were harvested

3. TERTIARY AROMAS

Wine improves with age. As do we. Or so we say, at any rate. Time in the barrel and time in the bottle allow aromas to develop in wine that would be otherwise impossible. Wine is able to develop and unfold over time. The tannins integrate into the wine and grow softer.

- **Bottle-aging**
  The aromas certain wines develop during a long, low-oxygen bottle-aging are some of the most exquisite and complex that wine can offer. Coarse tannins integrate gently into the wine, the initial acidity reduces, and the fruit aromas gain in complexity and develop into notes of ripe fruit, raisins, and spice.

There's a reason we romanticize drinking mature wines. After all, only a few bottles actually benefit from long cellaring. Only around 1 percent of all wines worldwide has the potential to age for over five years. Most wines currently sold for less than around thirty dollars are ready to drink right away. Wines for more than that price can well be left to age for up to five years. But of course, this is just a general rule of thumb—to which there are, obviously, exceptions.

From cellaring or bottle-aging

THE OVERALL IMPRESSION

At the end of a wine tasting, we often evaluate our overall impressions. In everyday life, we mainly do this when we take the first sip of a wine, whether at home or in a restaurant. What do I think of this wine? To put it very simply, there are two tendencies here.

- A good overall impression: This wine tastes good. It gives me the same feeling of happiness as a school exam being postponed.

- A bad overall impression: This wine doesn't taste good. I never want to see this wine ever again.

Here are the most important factors for a quick and concise evaluation:

Quality rating

- Is the wine clean, or is there something wrong with it? And by "clean" I mean that there are no flaws, not that it's spick-and-span.

Maturity

- Is it too young, still somewhat immature? But you just couldn't wait to open it? Better pour it into a decanter and aerate.

- Is it too old?—What took you so long? Decant it!

Overall assessment

- Positive: It's nicely concentrated: "full bodied, rich in essence." It's a well-balanced wine: The structural pillars (see page 38) are all at the same height.

- Negative: It's not concentrated: "thin, flat."

Finish

- The finish doesn't refer to your level of dignity after a lively evening over a bottle or two, but how long and how intensely the taste of a wine lingers on your palate after you've swallowed it. If the finish is hasty, abrupt, and flat, this can have a negative impact on the wine experience. If the finish is sustained, this boosts the wine quality considerably and it's just pure joy.

- Easy-drinking wines tend to have a short finish. These wines are fun for a free-and-easy drinks party, but they'll get their revenge the next morning (see page 24, hangover management).

Here are my best lines for showing off convincingly; clear messages always go down well.

"It's still a little closed in the nose but it clearly reveals intense concentration. Just needs to breathe a little longer."

"This is just the way I imagined this wine."

"Remarkable! The acidity is very present, yet it's an exceptionally well-balanced wine."

"The tannins have integrated beautifully here."

"Finally, a wine that reflects its terroir perfectly."

"An expressive wine. It will be outstanding once matured."

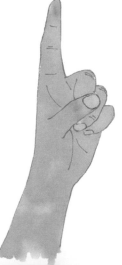

"It's rather young, but already fun at this stage."

"It's lacking a little in complexity, but it's a surefire crowd-pleaser."

Wine Growing

I remember the first time my mentor Lindsey took me out in a Jeep golf cart, up and down hills through the vineyards in Santa Ynez, California.

The earth was dry, the ground cracked. A warm wind was blowing; there was sand everywhere. Cactuses! I asked myself two questions: "Why do you want to work in a desert and not on the beach? And how on earth can grapes grow here?"

Thanks to my outspoken mentor, I soon learned: one, that I knew nothing, and two, that this was a unique terroir.

Since then, you could say I've learned a thing or two. It is my pleasure to introduce you now to the art of wine growing—terroir included.

TERROIR

No word in the entire wine world is spoken with greater reverence than *terroir*. Without terroir there is no wine. Without wine, there's no joy in life. Thus, terroir is joie de vivre.

Terroir is a complex subject that makes a lot of people rather uneasy—even triggers mild panic like a long line at security in an airport! Yet the principle is actually quite simple: It concerns the characteristics of any given place, what you might call the local flavor, which comes out in the wine.

Basically, the wine has taste characteristics that are influenced by the properties of the vineyard or the region. Think about it this way: We are also shaped by our environments. Just like how I, for example, tend to feel good in large groups because I grew up in a lively, noisy family.

These local characteristics are made up as follows.

- **Climate**
  The climate determines whether a grape variety will grow well in a certain place.

- **Terrain and soil**
  Provided the climate is suitable, the topographic structures (land surface), and especially the soil composition, play a decisive role in the character and quality of the resulting wine. This is why you can't just go and plant vines in the park next door.

Soil

- **Human influence**
Opinions differ on the question of how much influence the winemaker has on the terroir. Basically, the concept of terroir is easier to explain if you exclude the production process.

In the words of Jeffrey Grosset, founder of Grosset Wines in Clare Valley, Australia: "I don't see winemaking as part of terroir, but rather that poor winemaking can interfere with its expression and good winemaking can allow pure expression."

Let's hope and trust that the winemaker interferes as little as possible in the terroir, and leave their influence aside here to concentrate predominantly on climate, terrain, and soil.

Climate

Terrain

CLIMATE

The average climate of a vineyard determines the grapes that can thrive there and the whole growing season of the vines, too—from the first blossom to the ripened grape.

Since the climate can also be responsible for entire harvests failing, this partially explains the high price of certain wines. These include Burgundies and Champagnes, which benefit from premium soil properties but also often face difficult weather conditions.

How climate affects the grapes

- **Sun**
  Like people, grapes also thrive better in the sun. The warmer the weather, the more sugar and aromas the grapes will produce. They ripen fully, which makes for concentrated wine. But too much sun can also lead to very high-alcohol wines. In the worst case, the grape simply gives up and doesn't even ripen at all.

Warmth

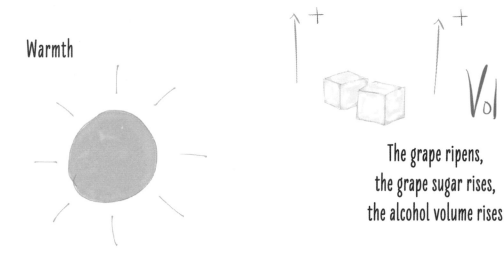

The grape ripens,
the grape sugar rises,
the alcohol volume rises

- **Clouds**
  The cooler the weather, the more sharpness remains in the grapes, and the crisper and fresher the wine will end up. After all, grapes can also ripen in cloudy yet warm conditions. For good results, you need sugar and acidity to be well balanced.

- **Wind**
  Wind combats frost, which can cause poor harvests, and prevents grapes from rotting after rain. The wind has a drying effect—like a blow-dryer.

Cool temperature

Creates acidity in the grapes

Wind

Drying combats frost, prevents rot

TERRAIN

Terrain has the same significance for winemakers as the mantra "location, location, location" for real-estate agents. Location is everything.

Imagine that you buy your dream house. You rearrange the floor plan slightly and renovate. It's perfect, so you move in. But you hadn't noticed that it's under a flight path. It's the right house, but in the wrong place.

It's the same with vineyards. The winemaker can change the way the grapes are trained; fertilize; plant trees and bushes to increase biodiversity; or even go to the exaggerated lengths of installing patio heaters. But if the plot is in a basin that's wreathed in fog 365 days a year, even the mightiest efforts are doomed to failure.

How terrain affects the grapes

- **Altitude**
  Vineyards at high altitudes benefit from hot days (sugar formation) and cool nights (acidity), which have a positive effect on the ripening of the grapes. Because cold air is heavier than warm air, it settles in lower-lying areas. The associated dampness can cause diseases such as mildew on the grapes. At higher altitudes, the grapes are protected from this.

- **Topography**
  Slopes encourage water to run off, while standing water in the soil in flat areas limits the ability of the vine's root system to take up nutrients.

- **Direction**
  In dry, warmer areas the most favorable slopes face southeast to eastward (the grapes need less sun), while in rainier, cooler places, south- to southwest-facing slopes are better (the grapes need more sun here).

- **Bodies of water**
  Through their heat-storage capacity (water cools more slowly than air), bodies of water give off heat; this rises uphill as warm air. This is particularly beneficial in winter and spring, as it helps the grapes to ripen and protects them from frost.

By contrast, as cold air is heavier than warm air, it flows down the slopes of a vineyard at night and in cooler weather. This cooling effect is particularly important in summer for the acid levels in the grapes. By day, the air is then warmed by the water, and the whole cycle begins again.

Thermals balance out extremes of temperature

50°F
(10°C)

60°F (15°C)

Cold air cools the surrounding area and helps build acidity.

The water acts as a heat reservoir and warms the area, ensuring that the grapes ripen.

SOIL

How soil affects the grapes

Wine experts are obsessed with soil. Like toddlers in a sandbox, nothing fascinates them more than messing around with dirt. Except, they are searching for something else. Kids might be hunting for worms, but the wine experts are on a quest for the perfect soil composition.

If the climate and terrain are right, the prerequisites for a good wine are there. Worldwide, there are plenty of places with acceptable conditions to make drinkable wine. But the optimal soil composition is the factor that separates the wheat from the chaff. This, by the way, is the main reason why some wines are so expensive: There just aren't many spots on the globe with such outstanding soil quality.

Wine specialists will debate whether there's a connection between the chemical composition of the soil and the aromas in wine with the same emotional intensity as people who insist smooth is better than chunky peanut butter.

There is no doubt, however, that the physical components of the soil, which affect the grapes via the water supply, influence the quality and structure of the wine.

What makes outstanding soil?

The most important and most valuable characteristics of suitable soil are good drainage, good water retention, and sufficient aerated space in the ground. This is because waterlogging will kill vines.

Next to water, vines love nitrogen, which helps the shoots and grapes to grow. But with too much nitrogen, the shoots and leaves go nuts and grow rampantly all over the place. Other minerals that vines love include phosphorus, potassium, sulfur, magnesium, and calcium.

THE ALLURE OF MUD

Organic material

Minerals and humus

Clay, loam, sand

Weathered stone
Bedrock

The most important layer for a
wine's character

Good drainage but enough water reserves

pH Acidity in the soil makes the minerals more
readily accessible

↓ Optimum root depth: 3 feet (1 m) +

 Enough nitrogen for photosynthesis

Tasting soil

You can taste soil in a very rudimentary way: Pick up a stone from the ground. Put your tongue out. Lick.

Or, to put it slightly more professionally: Wines from different soils (plots) taste differently. Whether a rock like granite, for example—which has strength and energy—passes its flavor on to the vine and hence to the wine is subject to further discussion. It's a tricky topic. But it's certainly true that if you plant the same kind of grape in two different soils, you will get two different wines. Burgundy is a perfect example: Clay soils give the pinot noir depth, while limestone makes for good structure.

The relationships between rock types and taste can be laid out as follows.

Good to know

The roots of old vines (twenty years old or more) can reach down as far as 65 feet (20 m) deep. Their root network is so well developed to enable them to take up a variety of minerals. Wines from old vines often feel silkier on the palate and have a perceptible depth and multifaceted, complex nature.

THE STONE TRIANGLE

Some of the most common vineyard soils

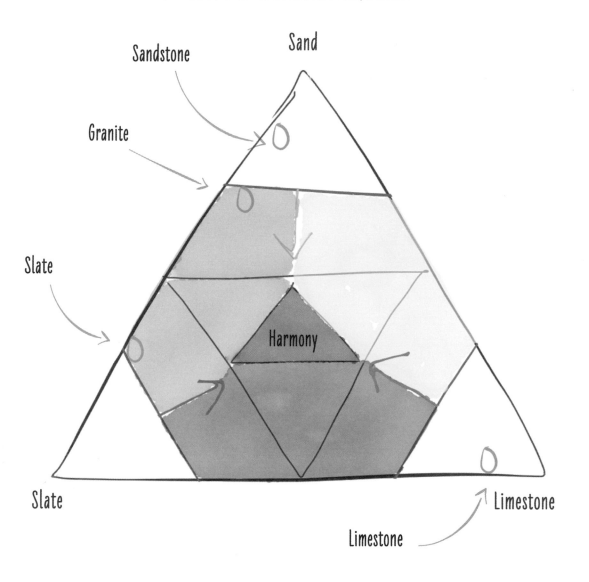

Sandstone

Granite

Sand

Slate

Harmony

Slate

Limestone

Limestone

WHEN THINGS GET ROCKY

How soils shape—and are tasted—in wine

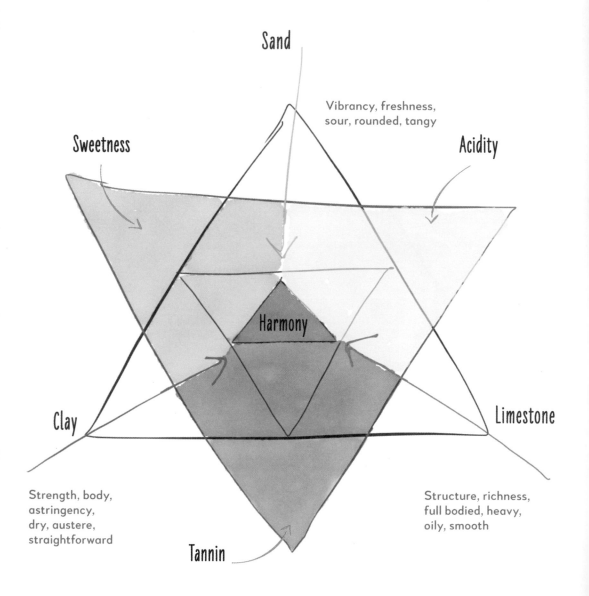

Sand

Vibrancy, freshness, sour, rounded, tangy

Sweetness

Acidity

Harmony

Clay

Limestone

Strength, body, astringency, dry, austere, straightforward

Structure, richness, full bodied, heavy, oily, smooth

Tannin

Graphite

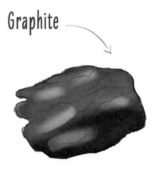

What is meant by a "mineral" aroma?

Minerality refers to the way we perceive the taste of the rock in the soil on our palate. It's hard to describe the perception of minerality because it means something different to everyone. To me, it means freshness.

I use the aroma descriptions "minerality" or "mineral" to describe a wine when I mean neither fruit, acidity, tannins, alcohol, nor sugar, and I sense nothing animal, spicy, or herbal about it either.

Minerality can be described as a lively kick of freshness—something like a breath mint, without the sharpness that brings tears to your eyes.

Iodine

Chalk

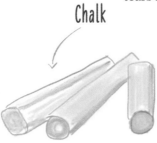

Breath mints

Wet stone

THE LIFE OF A VINE

The second most important factor after the terroir is the work of the winemaker. The specific process can vary quite a lot from winemaker to winemaker, so I have simplified it, and the stages in the development of a vine, to just the basics in the following section. Allow me to compare the life cycle of the vine with something we know inside out: our own life.

1. Haircut

For a vine, the year begins with a "haircut." In January or February, almost all the shoots from the previous year, known as the old wood, are cut back (pruned), leaving only one or two. This is how the quantity of grapes per vine is defined (reduced), which strongly influences the wine quality. Less is more.

2. Tears of joy

As the days grow warmer in March or April, the vines begin to "weep" with joy: Sap pushes its way out where the shoots have been pruned (see below), a sign that the annual growth cycle is getting started. This is where the buds will form later. The shoots are fastened (trained) to wires so they don't grow like tropical vines in a jungle.

TEARS OF JOY
March, April

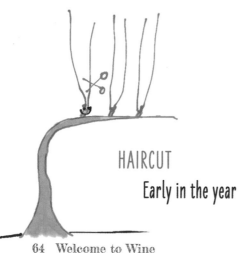

HAIRCUT
Early in the year

3. Party poppers

At the end of April, the little buds burst out from the woody shoots. If the weather is very warm, this can be almost explosive.

GROWTH SPURT
May, June

PARTY POPPER
Late April

4. Growth spurt

In around May, the buds develop clusters, which eventually blossom into small white flowers in June. They are self-fertilizing—the male pollen grains fall on the female egg cells in the ovaries—and the pollinated blossoms develop into small berries, which look like frozen peas: small, green, and hard. There's no stopping them now; the shoots grow rampantly and wildly.

5. Starting school

In July the vines "start school." The young shoots need training (using a trellis system): The wine-grower puts them in their place so that they grow in a controlled manner. If the shoots grow too long, they need to be cut back so that the vine doesn't waste energy on growth and can invest it in the grapes instead. It's as though the vine has to be constantly reminded of its main job, i.e., delivering top-quality grapes rather than greenery that can't be pressed or drunk.

By now, the grapes have reached a certain size. The first berry bunches are already being cut out so as to reduce the yield: quality over quantity. The shoots are, in a way, being taught to concentrate.

6. Teenage phase

In August, the grapes start to rebel: They change color as they start to ripen (*veraison* sets in). White wine grapes turn yellower, red wine varieties go bluer. Like a teenager, each grape develops in its own time, depending on the variety and whether it's had more sun or more shade.

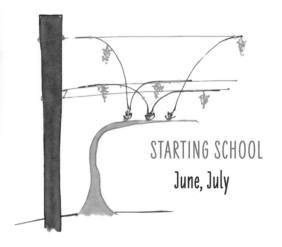

STARTING SCHOOL
June, July

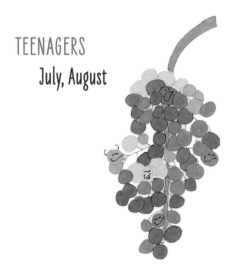

TEENAGERS
July, August

7. Final exams

From now on it's all about the ripening. The sugar content of the grapes increases with the warm days, and the acidity declines steadily. The moment of truth—exactly the right time to harvest so as to maintain the acidity in a perfectly ripe grape with enough sugar—is for the winemakers to decide, on the basis of their experience. A gadget called a refractometer is handy here: This measures the must weight (sugar content) of the grape juice, from which the potential alcohol content can be determined.

The harvest is usually done in September and/or October.

8. Quitting time

After the harvest, the leaves fall and the vines go into hibernation. They pretty much play dead, before the whole thing starts over again in the new year.

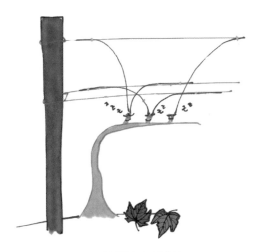

AFTER WORK
End of the Year

FINAL EXAMS
September

GRAPE VARIETIES

There are several thousand grape varieties around the world. Of course, this is no help at all in trying to get an overview of the wine world. It's worth repeating: The more you learn about wine, the more you realize you barely know anything.

But don't be discouraged! Here come the key grape varieties, subdivided by eight different wine styles. I've also listed the major aromas, but don't worry if you've never smelled some of these things. Some of them are pretty far-fetched, and there's a reason for the motto: "Learning by drinking." And there are always exceptions.

To help you remember the grape varieties, I've given each of them a distinguishing trait, too.

MILD AND ROUND

CHARDONNAY
Trait: eclectic
Character in cool climates: citrusy, dry, mineral, like Helen Mirren in *The Queen*
Aromas: apples and pears
Growing regions: Chablis, Burgundy, Champagne (France); Austria; Oregon (USA)

Character in warm climates: lush, rich, voluminous as Beyoncé's hair being blown by a wind machine
Aromas: buttery, nutty, honey, secondary aromas (vanilla)
Growing regions: California; Chile; Hunter Region and Victoria (Australia); Hawke's Bay and Wairarapa (New Zealand)

CHASSELAS, GUTEDEL
Trait: down-to-earth
Character: well-balanced, neutral as a Swiss citizen
Aromas: mineral, citrusy, nutty, lime, lemon, grapefruit, peach, white pepper, spicy
Growing regions: Vaud, Geneva (Switzerland); Markgräflerland (Germany)

GARNACHA BLANCA

Trait: soft
Character: velvety, charming, accessible, like Matthew McConaughey's accent
Aromas: grapefruit, gooseberries, kiwi, pear
Growing regions: Navarra, Priorat, Tarragona, La Mancha, Aragon (all in Spain)

GRAUBURGUNDER, PINOT GRIGIO, PINOT GRIS

Trait: flattering
General Character: refreshing, lively, and dashing as James Bond
Character: juicy, complex, fresh
Aromas: citrus, pear, almonds
Growing regions: Rheinhessen, Pfalz, Baden, Nahe (Germany); Switzerland

Pinot Grigio

Character: light, crisp, dry
Aromas: citrusy (lemon, lime), apple, floral
Growing regions: Veneto, Friuli-Venezia Giulia, South Tyrol (Italy)

Pinot Gris

Character: richer, sometimes semisweet
Aromas: stone fruit (peach, nectarine), citrus, floral (honeysuckle)
Growing regions: Alsace (France), Valais (Switzerland), Oregon (USA)

CRISP AND FRESH

GRÜNER VELTLINER

Trait: perky
Character: refreshing, crisp, peppery like Cardi B
Aromas: lime, lemon, grapefruit, peach, white pepper, spicy
Growing regions: Weinviertel, Wagram, Kremstal, Kamptal (practically all of Austria); Czech Republic; Slovenia; Hungary

ARNEIS

Trait: cheerful
Character: perky and crowd-pleasing like pop music
Aromas: citrus, green fruits (pear), stone fruit (apricot), floral (white blossom, chamomile), nutty (almonds)
Growing regions: Roero and Langhe in Piedmont (Italy)

SAUVIGNON BLANC

Trait: refreshing

Character: crisp, fresh, and appealing as a face mask on Sunday morning

Aromas: citrus (lemon, lime)

Growing regions: Sancerre, Pouilly-sur-Loire, Bordeaux (France); Switzerland; Austria; New Zealand; USA

VERDEJO

Trait: rousing

Character: light, delicate and soft, like Enrique Iglesias in his song "Hero"

Aromas: citrus (lemon), herbal (fennel, anise)

Growing regions: Rueda (Spain)— wines named "Rueda" consist of at least 50 percent verdejo, the rest is sauvignon blanc and macabeo.

POWERFUL AND EXPRESSIVE

CHENIN BLANC

Trait: hyperactive

Character: lively, light, proud, complicated—and can be made in a range of styles from sweet to dry, like a young Miley Cyrus

Aromas: green fruits (pear), exotic fruits (passion fruit), herbal (ginger)

Growing regions: Loire (France): dry to sweet; South Africa: only dry

Also used for sparkling wine production: Crémant de Loire (Loire Valley, France), Crémant de Limoux (Languedoc, France)

GEWÜRZTRAMINER

Trait: aromatic

Character: powerful, spicy, tropical, exotic and sometimes semisweet, like Tom Hanks in *Cast Away*

Aromas: tropical fruits (lychee, grapefruit, mango, pineapple), floral (rose), honey, candied fruits

Growing regions: Baden, Pfalz (Germany); Alsace (France); Austria; Hungary; Australia; South Tyrol (Italy)

RIESLING
Trait: proud
Character: straightforward, intense and proud as a patriot
Aromas: stone fruit (peach), green fruits (apple), citrus (lemon), mineral, honey
Growing regions: Pfalz, Mosel, Rheinhessen (Germany): from dry to sweet; Alsace (France): just dry; Washington State (USA)
Styles: *Prädikatswein*, kabinett, spätlese

VERMENTINO
Trait: hearty
Character: invigorating, light, and playful, like Forrest Gump
Aromas: pineapple, grapefruit, nutty (almonds), mineral
Growing regions: Sardinia, Tuscany (Italy)

LUSH AND FULL

MOSCATO D'ASTI
Trait: extroverted
Character: lush, seductive, floral, and a little bit crisp, like Madonna's outfits
Aromas: stone fruit (peach, nectarine), citrus (lemon), floral (jasmine, rose, orange blossom), honey
Growing regions: Asti in Piedmont (Italy)

VIOGNIER
Trait: vivacious
Character: ripe, lush, and soft as a baby's face
Aromas: stone fruit (peach), tropical fruits (melon, lychee), citrus (lemon, mandarin), floral (rose, honeysuckle, acacia)
Growing regions: Rhône Valley (France); USA; Australia

RED GRAPE VARIETIES

LIGHT AND SOFT

GAMAY
Trait: friendly
Character: light, uncomplicated, and playful, like a typical Jennifer Aniston character
Aromas: black fruit (black currants), red fruit (raspberries), floral (violets), earthy
Growing regions: Beaujolais, Burgundy, Loire (France); Switzerland

GRENACHE
Trait: cheery
Character: soft, a little bit sharp with a sweet mellowness, like Ed Sheeran
Aromas: red fruit (raspberries, strawberries), spicy (pepper, cinnamon)
Growing regions: Châteauneuf-du-Pape, Languedoc-Roussillon (France); Navarra, Rioja (Spain); Australia; USA

PINOT NOIR
Trait: elegant
Character: delicate, complex, seductive, like the cosmetics range of Kardashian & co.
Aromas: red fruit (strawberries, raspberries, cherries), spicy (nutmeg)
Growing regions: Burgundy, Champagne (France); Switzerland (also known as blauburgunder); Germany (known as spätburgunder); Oregon, California (USA); New Zealand

BLAUER PORTUGIESER
Trait: hip
Character: light, fragrant, and accessible, like a puppy
Aromas: red fruit (cherries, red currants), spicy (vanilla)
Growing regions: Rheinhessen, Pfalz (Germany); Retz, Thermenregion, Burgenland (Austria); Slovenia

ROUND AND SOFT

CARMENÈRE
Trait: profound
Character: rich, austere and complex, like Mumford & Sons' songs
Aromas: black fruit (black currants, blackberries), red fruit (cherries), spicy (chocolate), herbal (green peppers, black pepper), earthy (tobacco, leather)
Growing regions: Bordeaux (France); Chile; New Zealand; China

MERLOT
Trait: cuddly
Character: soft, velvety, and crowd-pleasing, like a box of gourmet chocolates
Aromas: black fruit (plums, blueberries, blackberries), red fruit (cherries), herbal (peppermint), earthy (leather)
Growing regions: Ticino (Switzerland); Bordeaux, Languedoc-Roussillon (France); Italy; South Africa; Chile; Argentina; Washington State, California (USA)

TEMPRANILLO
Trait: collegial
Character: juicy, vegetal, and leathery, like Johnny Depp's perfume
Aromas: black fruit (plums), red fruit (cherries), floral (violets), spicy (vanilla, toast), earthy (leather, tobacco)
Growing regions: Douro, Alentejo (Portugal); Rioja, Ribera del Duero, Penedès, Navarra (Spain); USA; Argentina; Chile

ZWEIGELT
Trait: strong
Character: powerful, concentrated, and harmonious, like Roger Federer's tennis style
Aromas: red fruit (cherries, red currants), spicy (vanilla)
Growing regions: Neusiedlersee, Carnuntum, Göttlesbrunn (Austria); Saale-Unstrut, Württemberg, Franconia (Germany)

HEARTY AND POWERFUL

BARBERA
Trait: robust
Character: robust, juicy, lively, like a Woody Allen film
Aromas: red fruit (cherries), black fruit (blackberries), herbal (rosemary), spicy (pepper), earthy (tobacco)
Growing regions: Piedmont, Emilia-Romagna, Lombardy (Italy); California, Oregon (USA); Mendoza, San Juan (Argentina)

BLAUFRÄNKISCH
Trait: crowd-pleasing
Character: refreshing, full, and charming, like Bill Murray in *Lost in Translation*
Aromas: black fruit (plums, blackberries), herbal (eucalyptus, bay leaf), spicy (pepper, chocolate), mineral
Growing regions: Burgenland, Neusiedlersee, Carnuntum (Austria); Hungary; Croatia; Czech Republic; Washington State (USA)

CABERNET FRANC
Trait: jolly
Character: charming, peppery, and flirtatious, like Reese Witherspoon
Aromas: red fruit (raspberries, cherries, red currants), herbal (eucalyptus), mineral
Growing regions: Bordeaux, Touraine/ Loire, southwest France (France); northeast Italy; Albania; Australia

CABERNET SAUVIGNON
Trait: muscular
Character: powerful, sensual and well structured, like David Beckham's pecs
Aromas: black fruit (blackberries, blueberries), herbal (paprika, peppermint), spicy (vanilla, chocolate, smoky, cedar), earthy (tobacco, leather, graphite)
Growing regions: Bordeaux (France); Washington State, California (USA); Tuscany (Italy); Lebanon; Israel; Chile; China

MALBEC

Trait: juicy

Character: sensual, robust and juicy, like Lady Gaga's steak dress

Aromas: black fruit (plums, blackberries, blueberries), floral (violets), herbal (tomato, oregano, thyme), spicy (vanilla, chocolate, smoky), earthy (tobacco, leather)

Growing regions: Mendoza (Argentina); Bordeaux, southwest France, Cahors (France); Chile; Australia

MONTEPULCIANO

Trait: seductive

Character: profound, solid, and rich, like Tolstoy's *War and Peace*

Aromas: red fruit (cherries), black fruit (plums, black currants), herbal (oregano), spicy (pepper, cloves), earthy (tar)

Growing regions: Abruzzo, Marche, Puglia (Italy); New Zealand; USA

NEBBIOLO

Trait: self-confident

Character: intense, robust, and complex, like George Clooney

Aromas: red fruit (cherries), black fruit (plums), floral (violets), spicy (vanilla, licorice), herbal, earthy (truffle, leather, tobacco)

Growing regions: Valtellina, Barolo, Barbaresco (Italy); California, Oregon, Washington State (USA); Mexico; Chile; Australia

PINOTAGE

Trait: bold

Character: lively, bold, and concentrated, like Serena Williams

Aromas: red fruit (cherries), dark fruit (blackberries, figs), herbal (menthol), spicy, secondary aromas (smoky, vanilla)

Growing regions: South Africa

SANGIOVESE

Trait: chic

Character: elegant, robust, and multifaceted, like Angelina Jolie

Aromas: red fruit (strawberries, cherries), black fruit (plums, figs), herbal (tomato, oregano, thyme), earthy (tobacco, leather, clay)

Growing regions: Montalcino, Montepulciano, and Chianti in Tuscany, Umbria, Emilia-Romagna (Italy); Corsica (France); California, Washington State (USA); Australia

TOURIGA NACIONAL

Trait: intense

Character: intense, solid, and powerful, like the voice of Aretha Franklin

Aromas: dark fruit (plums, blackberries, black currants), herbal (peppermint), spicy (licorice)

Growing regions: Douro, Dão, Alentejo (Portugal); South Africa

LUSH AND FULL

NERO D'AVOLA

Trait: full-flavored

Character: powerful, expansive and velvety, like Tom Brady

Aromas: red fruit (plums, black cherries), cassis, spicy

Growing regions: Sicily, Sardinia (Italy)

SYRAH / SHIRAZ

Trait: ambiguous

Character: velvety, multilayered, and concentrated, like Adele's voice

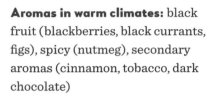

Aromas in warm climates: black fruit (blackberries, black currants, figs), spicy (nutmeg), secondary aromas (cinnamon, tobacco, dark chocolate)

Growing regions in warm climates: Barossa Valley (Australia); Italy; South Africa; Chile

Aromas in cool climates: black fruit (blackberries, mulberries, black currants), herbal (juniper), spicy (pepper, licorice), secondary aromas (smoke)

Growing regions in cool climates: Hermitage, Côte-Rôtie, Saint Joseph, Châteauneuf-du-Pape in southern France (France); Walla Walla in Washington State, California (USA)

ZINFANDEL/ PRIMITIVO

Trait: illuminating

Character: jammy, lush, and lithe, like everything Oprah Winfrey says

Aromas: black fruit (figs, blackberries), spicy (cloves, pepper, chocolate), secondary aromas (cinnamon)

Growing regions: Puglia (Italy); California (USA); Croatia

WINE REGIONS

In the section on terroir you learned why you can't get good wine by planting a vine in a flower pot on the balcony. There are a lot of conditions to be met if you want to produce an even halfway pleasant wine.

The best conditions for vines can be found between 40 and 50 degrees latitude in the Northern Hemisphere, and between 30 and 40 degrees latitude in the Southern Hemisphere.

Or that's the case at the moment, anyway. We'll have to wait and see where grapes can be grown in thirty years' time because of global warming. ("Käsivarren erämaa-alue" in Finland sounds like it could be a renowned wine region one day!)

Long story short: In this section, I'll introduce you to major wine-growing regions.

FRANCE

The country where terroir matters more than politics

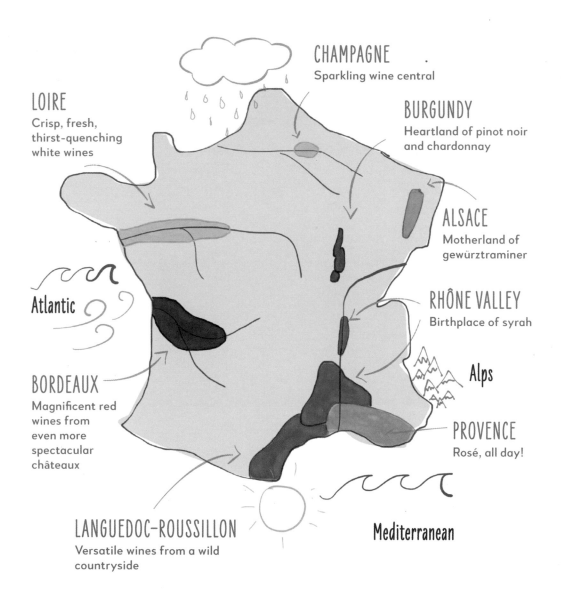

CHAMPAGNE
Sparkling wine central

LOIRE
Crisp, fresh, thirst-quenching white wines

BURGUNDY
Heartland of pinot noir and chardonnay

ALSACE
Motherland of gewürztraminer

Atlantic

RHÔNE VALLEY
Birthplace of syrah

Alps

BORDEAUX
Magnificent red wines from even more spectacular châteaux

PROVENCE
Rosé, all day!

LANGUEDOC-ROUSSILLON
Versatile wines from a wild countryside

Mediterranean

BORDEAUX

Realm of legendary tannins and epic cellaring potential

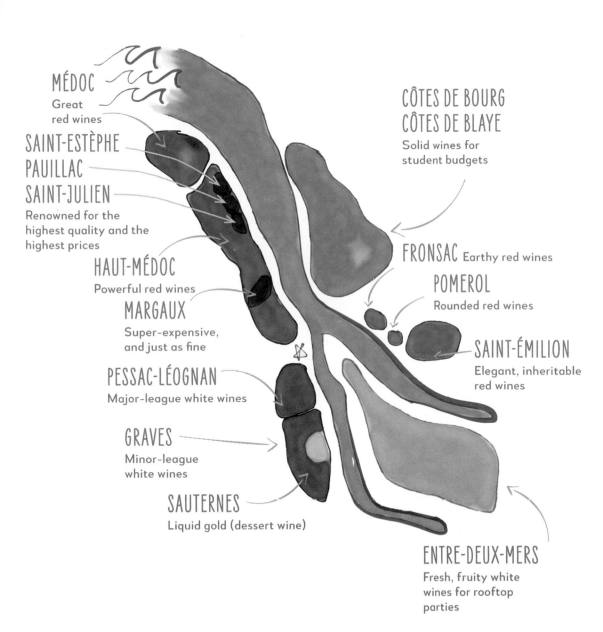

MÉDOC
Great
red wines

**SAINT-ESTÈPHE
PAUILLAC
SAINT-JULIEN**
Renowned for the
highest quality and the
highest prices

HAUT-MÉDOC
Powerful red wines

MARGAUX
Super-expensive,
and just as fine

PESSAC-LÉOGNAN
Major-league white wines

GRAVES
Minor-league
white wines

SAUTERNES
Liquid gold (dessert wine)

**CÔTES DE BOURG
CÔTES DE BLAYE**
Solid wines for
student budgets

FRONSAC Earthy red wines

POMEROL
Rounded red wines

SAINT-ÉMILION
Elegant, inheritable
red wines

ENTRE-DEUX-MERS
Fresh, fruity white
wines for rooftop
parties

BURGUNDY

The realm of the most complex and unpronounceable wines

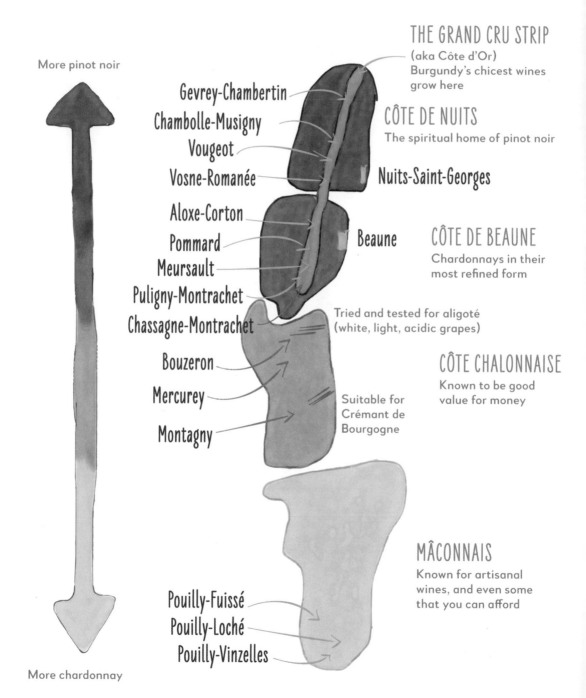

More pinot noir

Gevrey-Chambertin
Chambolle-Musigny
Vougeot
Vosne-Romanée

Aloxe-Corton
Pommard
Meursault
Puligny-Montrachet
Chassagne-Montrachet

Bouzeron
Mercurey
Montagny

Pouilly-Fuissé
Pouilly-Loché
Pouilly-Vinzelles

More chardonnay

THE GRAND CRU STRIP
(aka Côte d'Or)
Burgundy's chicest wines
grow here

CÔTE DE NUITS
The spiritual home of pinot noir

Nuits-Saint-Georges

Beaune

CÔTE DE BEAUNE
Chardonnays in their
most refined form

Tried and tested for aligoté
(white, light, acidic grapes)

CÔTE CHALONNAISE
Known to be good
value for money

Suitable for
Crémant de
Bourgogne

MÂCONNAIS
Known for artisanal
wines, and even some
that you can afford

ITALY

Vines wherever you look

SOUTH TYROL
Lively white wines and dry reds, for connoisseurs and wannabe connoisseurs

FRIULI
Luxury white wines

The Alps   Switzerland   Grüezi!

PIEDMONT
Red wines for aging and sweet moscato d'Asti

VENETO
Where prosecco rubs shoulders with amarone

TUSCANY
Italy's "big player"

EMILIA-ROMAGNA
Fizzy joy in a bottle. Forza lambrusco!

ABRUZZO
Rustic red wines

CORSICA
Part of France

Vineyards here

PUGLIA
Primitivo as far as the eye can see

Mediterranean

Vineyards there

CAMPANIA
The aglianico grape in top form

SARDINIA
Rounded, full-bodied red and white wines

Vineyards everywhere

SICILY
Known for red wines, and especially famous for sweet Marsala

PIEDMONT

Italian paradise: cult wines and truffles

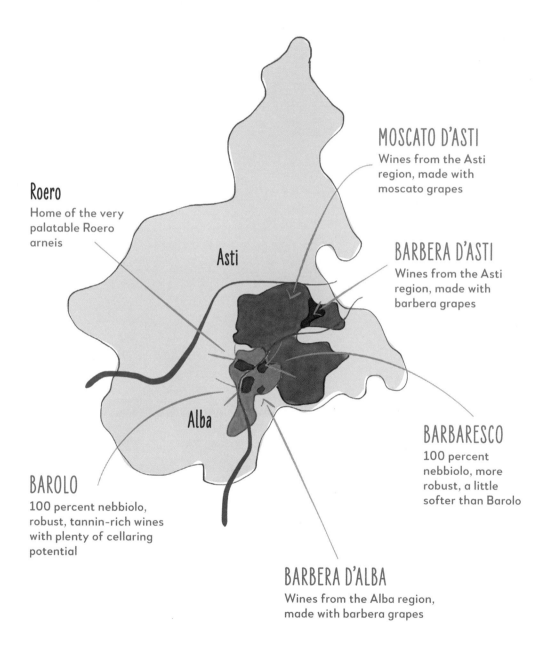

MOSCATO D'ASTI
Wines from the Asti region, made with moscato grapes

BARBERA D'ASTI
Wines from the Asti region, made with barbera grapes

Roero
Home of the very palatable Roero arneis

Asti

BARBARESCO
100 percent nebbiolo, more robust, a little softer than Barolo

Alba

BAROLO
100 percent nebbiolo, robust, tannin-rich wines with plenty of cellaring potential

BARBERA D'ALBA
Wines from the Alba region, made with barbera grapes

TUSCANY

Italy's most self-confident wines

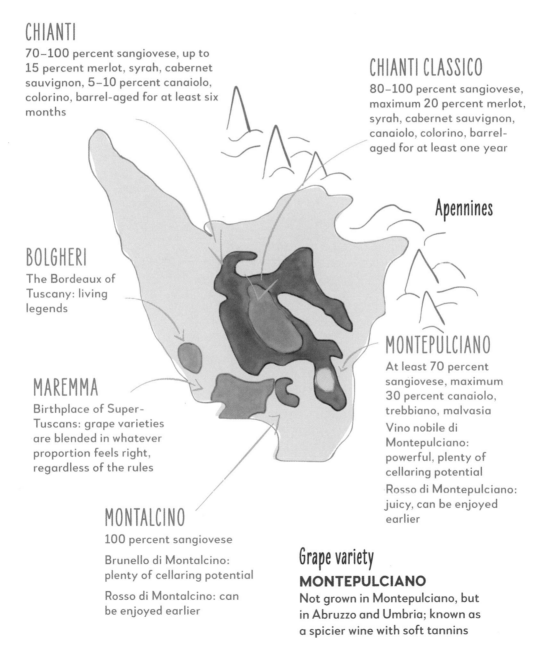

CHIANTI

70–100 percent sangiovese, up to 15 percent merlot, syrah, cabernet sauvignon, 5–10 percent canaiolo, colorino, barrel-aged for at least six months

CHIANTI CLASSICO

80–100 percent sangiovese, maximum 20 percent merlot, syrah, cabernet sauvignon, canaiolo, colorino, barrel-aged for at least one year

Apennines

BOLGHERI

The Bordeaux of Tuscany: living legends

MONTEPULCIANO

At least 70 percent sangiovese, maximum 30 percent canaiolo, trebbiano, malvasia

Vino nobile di Montepulciano: powerful, plenty of cellaring potential

Rosso di Montepulciano: juicy, can be enjoyed earlier

MAREMMA

Birthplace of Super-Tuscans: grape varieties are blended in whatever proportion feels right, regardless of the rules

MONTALCINO

100 percent sangiovese

Brunello di Montalcino: plenty of cellaring potential

Rosso di Montalcino: can be enjoyed earlier

Grape variety
MONTEPULCIANO

Not grown in Montepulciano, but in Abruzzo and Umbria; known as a spicier wine with soft tannins

SPAIN

Tempranillo all over the map

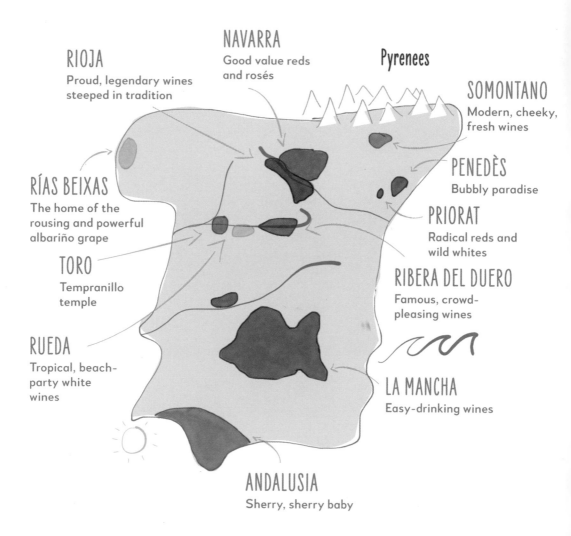

RIOJA
Proud, legendary wines steeped in tradition

NAVARRA
Good value reds and rosés

Pyrenees

SOMONTANO
Modern, cheeky, fresh wines

RÍAS BEIXAS
The home of the rousing and powerful albariño grape

PENEDÈS
Bubbly paradise

PRIORAT
Radical reds and wild whites

TORO
Tempranillo temple

RIBERA DEL DUERO
Famous, crowd-pleasing wines

RUEDA
Tropical, beach-party white wines

LA MANCHA
Easy-drinking wines

ANDALUSIA
Sherry, sherry baby

PORTUGAL

A kaleidoscope of colorful wines

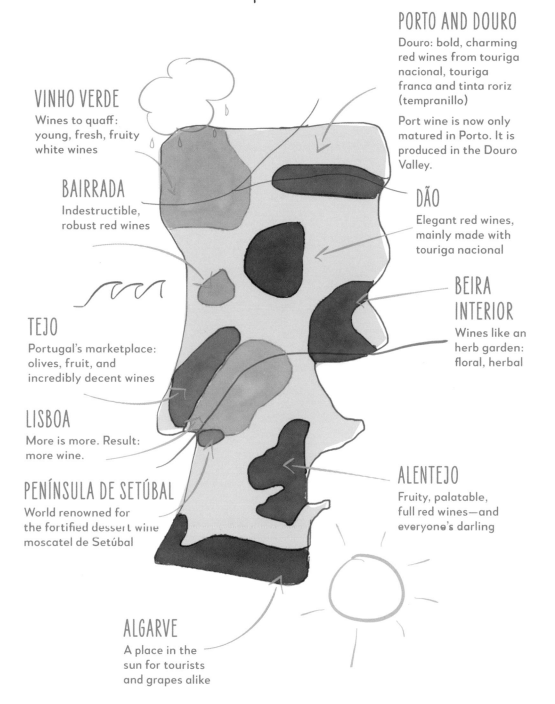

PORTO AND DOURO

Douro: bold, charming red wines from touriga nacional, touriga franca and tinta roriz (tempranillo)

Port wine is now only matured in Porto. It is produced in the Douro Valley.

VINHO VERDE

Wines to quaff: young, fresh, fruity white wines

BAIRRADA

Indestructible, robust red wines

DÃO

Elegant red wines, mainly made with touriga nacional

BEIRA INTERIOR

Wines like an herb garden: floral, herbal

TEJO

Portugal's marketplace: olives, fruit, and incredibly decent wines

LISBOA

More is more. Result: more wine.

ALENTEJO

Fruity, palatable, full red wines—and everyone's darling

PENÍNSULA DE SETÚBAL

World renowned for the fortified dessert wine moscatel de Setúbal

ALGARVE

A place in the sun for tourists and grapes alike

DOURO AND DUERO

A very, very important river that's home to lots and lots of grapes

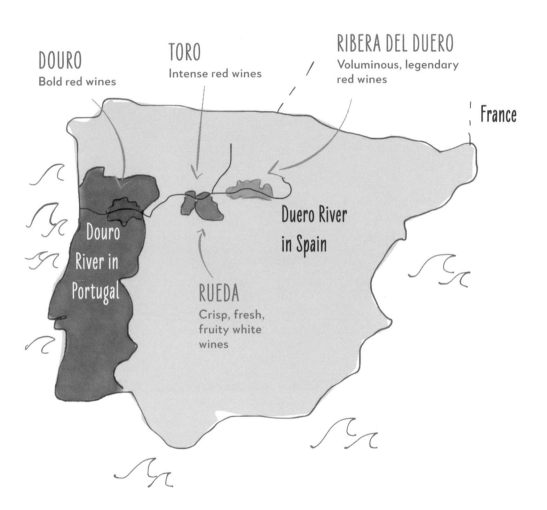

DOURO
Bold red wines

TORO
Intense red wines

RIBERA DEL DUERO
Voluminous, legendary
red wines

France

Douro
River in
Portugal

Duero River
in Spain

RUEDA
Crisp, fresh,
fruity white
wines

SWITZERLAND

Precision craftsmanship beyond watchmaking

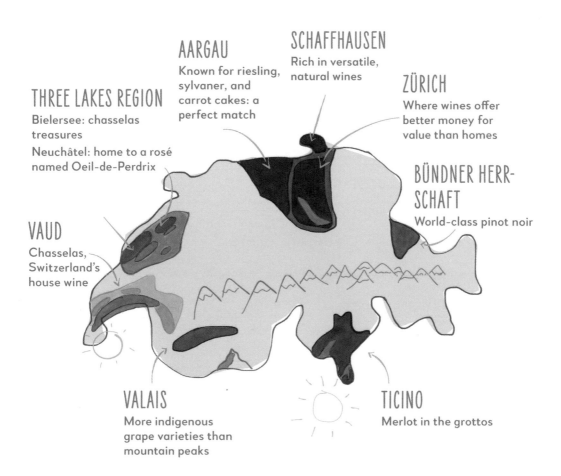

AARGAU
Known for riesling,
sylvaner, and
carrot cakes: a
perfect match

SCHAFFHAUSEN
Rich in versatile,
natural wines

ZÜRICH
Where wines offer
better money for
value than homes

THREE LAKES REGION
Bielersee: chasselas
treasures
Neuchâtel: home to a rosé
named Oeil-de-Perdrix

BÜNDNER HERR-SCHAFT
World-class pinot noir

VAUD
Chasselas,
Switzerland's
house wine

VALAIS
More indigenous
grape varieties than
mountain peaks

TICINO
Merlot in the grottos

AUSTRIA

Grüner veltliner republic

A WAGRAM
For self-discovery: substantial, hearty grüner veltliner

B TRAISENTAL
Fresh, fruity finesse

C WACHAU
Feel-good oasis for monumental white wines

D KREMSTAL
Dynamic region, known for white wines

E KAMPTAL
Austria's breath of fresh air: racy white wines with pronounced acidity

F THERMENREGION
Thermal springs and indigenous grapes that make you feel good inside and out

WEINVIERTEL
Peppery, cheeky gewürztraminer

CARNUNTUM
Known for regional wines and regional cuisine

NEUSIEDLERSEE
Oenological pampering: spoil yourself with the world's best sweet wines

LEITHABERG
Whiz kid of the wine regions: immense diversity

MITTELBURGENLAND
Austria's red wines

EISENBERG
Sassy blaufränkisch

VULKANLAND STEIERMARK
Extinct volcanos spark magnificent aromas

SÜDSTEIERMARK
(Southern Styria) refined sauvignon blanc

WESTSTEIERMARK
(Western Styria) known for schilcher rosé: wine made with the ancient Blauer Wildbacher grape

GERMANY

Riesling rules!

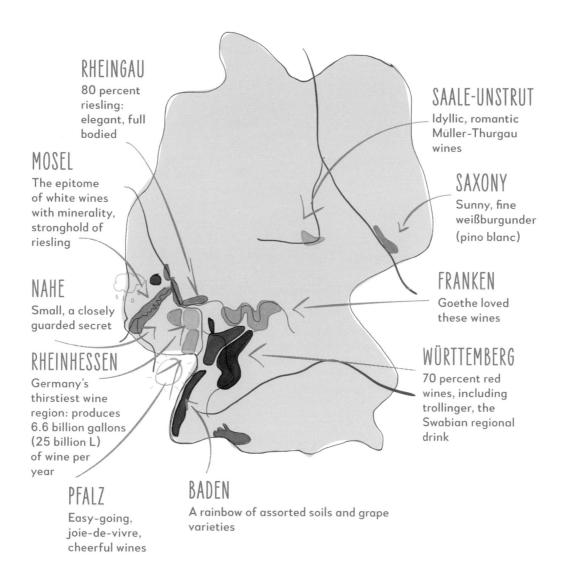

RHEINGAU
80 percent riesling: elegant, full bodied

MOSEL
The epitome of white wines with minerality, stronghold of riesling

NAHE
Small, a closely guarded secret

RHEINHESSEN
Germany's thirstiest wine region: produces 6.6 billion gallons (25 billion L) of wine per year

PFALZ
Easy-going, joie-de-vivre, cheerful wines

BADEN
A rainbow of assorted soils and grape varieties

SAALE-UNSTRUT
Idyllic, romantic Müller-Thurgau wines

SAXONY
Sunny, fine weißburgunder (pino blanc)

FRANKEN
Goethe loved these wines

WÜRTTEMBERG
70 percent red wines, including trollinger, the Swabian regional drink

ARGENTINA

Malbec, meat, call it a day

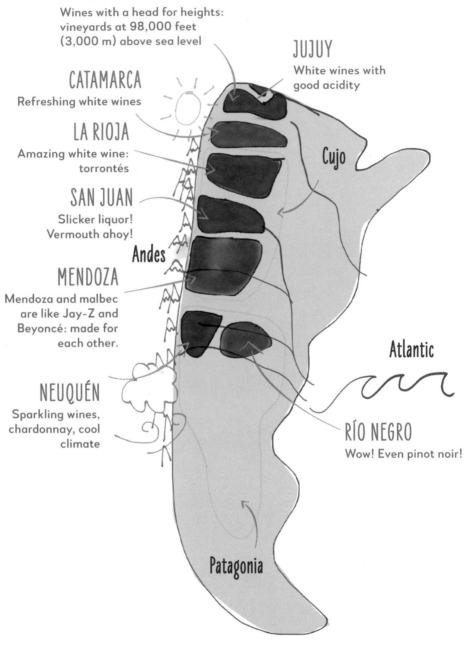

SALTA
Wines with a head for heights: vineyards at 98,000 feet (3,000 m) above sea level

JUJUY
White wines with good acidity

CATAMARCA
Refreshing white wines

LA RIOJA
Amazing white wine: torrontés

SAN JUAN
Slicker liquor! Vermouth ahoy!

MENDOZA
Mendoza and malbec are like Jay-Z and Beyoncé: made for each other.

NEUQUÉN
Sparkling wines, chardonnay, cool climate

Cujo

Andes

Atlantic

RÍO NEGRO
Wow! Even pinot noir!

Patagonia

CALIFORNIA

Flowers in your hair, the sea breeze on your face, the sun in your eyes

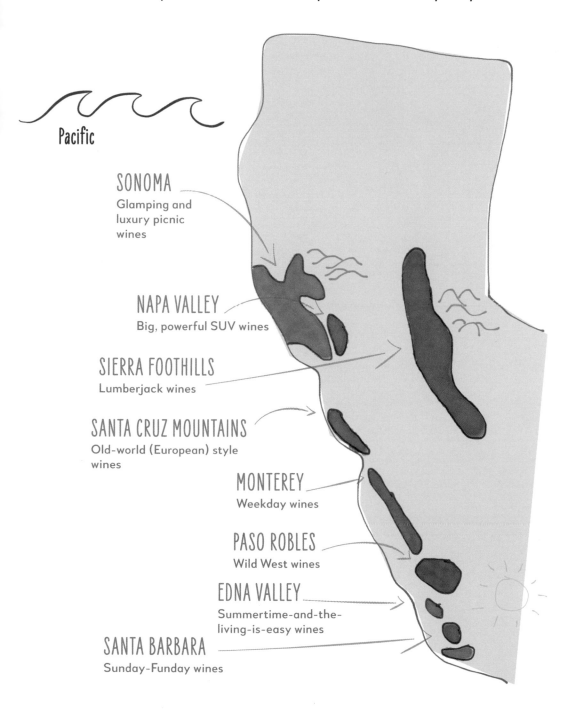

Pacific

SONOMA
Glamping and
luxury picnic
wines

NAPA VALLEY
Big, powerful SUV wines

SIERRA FOOTHILLS
Lumberjack wines

SANTA CRUZ MOUNTAINS
Old-world (European) style
wines

MONTEREY
Weekday wines

PASO ROBLES
Wild West wines

EDNA VALLEY
Summertime-and-the-
living-is-easy wines

SANTA BARBARA
Sunday-Funday wines

WASHINGTON

Where glaciers and vineyards coexist

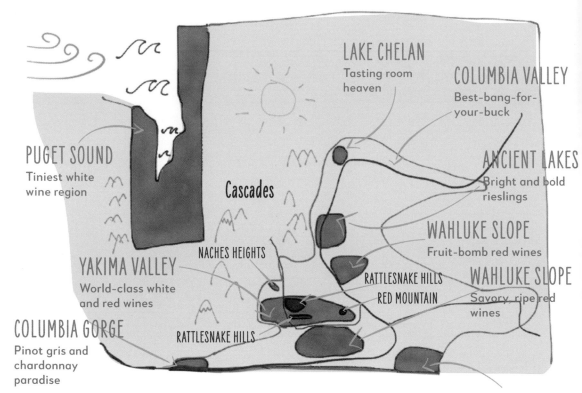

LAKE CHELAN
Tasting room heaven

COLUMBIA VALLEY
Best-bang-for-your-buck

PUGET SOUND
Tiniest white wine region

Cascades

ANCIENT LAKES
Bright and bold rieslings

WAHLUKE SLOPE
Fruit-bomb red wines

NACHES HEIGHTS

YAKIMA VALLEY
World-class white and red wines

RATTLESNAKE HILLS
RED MOUNTAIN

WAHLUKE SLOPE
Savory, ripe red wines

COLUMBIA GORGE
Pinot gris and chardonnay paradise

RATTLESNAKE HILLS

WALLA WALLA
One of *Vogue*'s "it" wine regions

OREGON

Volcanic mountains and textbook terroir

WILLIAMETTE VALLEY
Pinot noir kingdom

UMPQUA VALLEY
The white wine region:
pinot gris, sauvignon blanc,
gewürztraminer, and riesling

ROGUE VALLEY
For Rhône fans: syrah and viognier

SNAKE RIVER
Sunday-Funday
wines

AUSTRALIA

The epic razzmatazz of shiraz

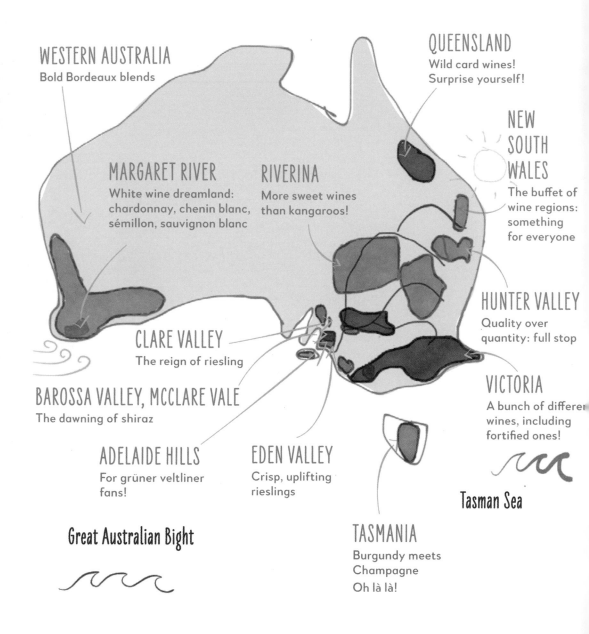

WESTERN AUSTRALIA
Bold Bordeaux blends

QUEENSLAND
Wild card wines!
Surprise yourself!

NEW SOUTH WALES
The buffet of wine regions: something for everyone

MARGARET RIVER
White wine dreamland: chardonnay, chenin blanc, sémillon, sauvignon blanc

RIVERINA
More sweet wines than kangaroos!

HUNTER VALLEY
Quality over quantity: full stop

CLARE VALLEY
The reign of riesling

BAROSSA VALLEY, MCCLARE VALE
The dawning of shiraz

VICTORIA
A bunch of differer wines, including fortified ones!

ADELAIDE HILLS
For grüner veltliner fans!

EDEN VALLEY
Crisp, uplifting rieslings

Tasman Sea

Great Australian Bight

TASMANIA
Burgundy meets Champagne
Oh là là!

BRITISH COLUMBIA

Putting Canada on the wine map (together with Ontario)

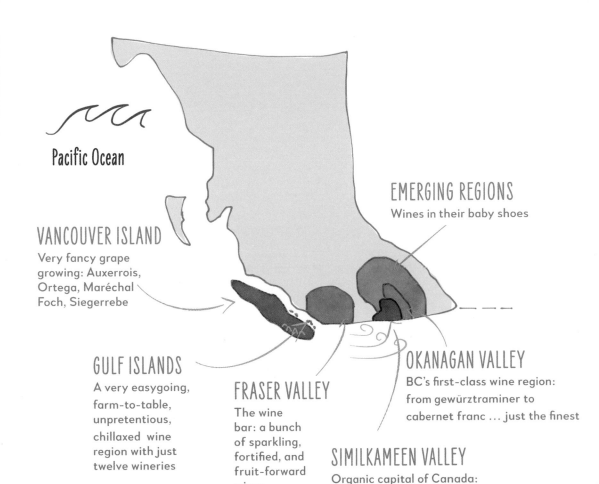

Pacific Ocean

EMERGING REGIONS
Wines in their baby shoes

VANCOUVER ISLAND
Very fancy grape growing: Auxerrois, Ortega, Maréchal Foch, Siegerrebe

GULF ISLANDS
A very easygoing, farm-to-table, unpretentious, chillaxed wine region with just twelve wineries

FRASER VALLEY
The wine bar: a bunch of sparkling, fortified, and fruit-forward wines

OKANAGAN VALLEY
BC's first-class wine region: from gewürztraminer to cabernet franc ... just the finest

SIMILKAMEEN VALLEY
Organic capital of Canada: known for bold red wines, chardonnay, and riesling

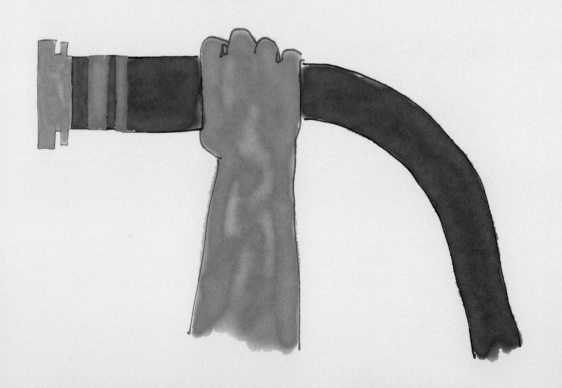

Winemaking

his chapter deals with the fine art of making wine and sparkling wine— one of the most exciting subjects when it comes to wine, because it involves both technical skill and a touch of magic: Ordinary grape juice with a little help from yeast becomes —ta-da!—wine.

Once the grapes arrive at the winery, the fate of the future wine lies in the hands of the winemaker. They decide how to produce their wine. Do they want to leave it as it is? Will they try to get the best out of the characteristics of the terroir, to show them off? Or will they shape it more subtly?

To give you a sense of all the factors involved, I'll walk you through the basic steps of the process. Trust me: You'll appreciate that glass of wine way more after this!

WINE PRODUCTION

Winemaking is a very complex business, so this is only intended as a very rudimentary, trimmed-down introduction to the key steps. All the same, it takes in quite a few technical aspects. Hold on tight!

STILL WINE

And I don't mean wine that hasn't turned into something else.... Still wines have no froth or fizz, because they contain very little or no carbon dioxide. Your normal wine, basically.

Here are the stages involved in their production.

Harvest and delivery: homecoming

The grapes may be harvested manually or by a machine. This decision is taken on grounds of cost, terrain, or the winemaker's philosophical approach. Manual harvesting means you can ensure that only healthy and ripe grapes are picked. After all, mistakes made at the beginning can't be corrected later.

The crop then comes into the winery. The grapes should be as fresh and intact as possible and shouldn't already have started to ferment in the harvesting baskets or crates.

Selection: casting

At this point, there is a further selection, depending on the winery's quality standards: Only healthy and ripe grapes will be processed further.

This is often done on a conveyor belt, in a process that calls for quick hands and sharp eyes. Ultra-modern wine producers even have machines to measure the density of the fruit and only select the ones that satisfy the target value for that particular grape variety.

Destemming: exposure

The stems are now removed, either by hand or by machine, because if they get into the wine, they'll bring rather unripe, woody, or tannic flavors with them. But for certain wine styles, the stems may be left on the grapes intentionally.

Maceration: goo

This step is mainly important for red wine. The grapes are crushed, creating a gooey mess of fruit pulp, seeds, skins, and juice, which is known as must. The must ends up in tanks or vats, in which the juice extracts tannins and dyes from the solid matter (the remains of the pulp, seeds, and skins). How much of them it takes up depends on how long the must is left to macerate, the temperature, and the enzyme activity. The longer it stands (the skins are in contact with the juice), the darker the wine and the more tannins it will contain.

Fermentation: yeast

As soon as the natural yeasts on the skins come into contact with the fructose in the pulp of the burst grapes, they transform it into alcohol and carbon dioxide. The carbon dioxide escapes from the open vat.

If the wine isn't to rely solely on the naturally occurring yeast, the winemaker can also add selected cultured yeast to the must.

The lower the fermentation temperature, the longer the fermentation will take, and the more gently the must (with red wines) or juice (with white wines) will ferment, encouraging a greater range of aromas. The alcoholic fermentation is complete when the yeast has no more sugar to consume or the temperature in the vat is lowered by the winemaker. Yeast is like us: It likes things warm and sweet—and keels over after too much alcohol or in the cold.

Pressing: Sunday morning

The must is pressed as lovingly as freshly squeezed orange juice on a Sunday morning. This separates the juice from the rest and is usually done with a pneumatic press: A horizontal balloon (membrane) inflates with air and presses the must against the wall of the round, cylinder-shaped press—nice and slowly and carefully, so that no bitter compounds are pressed out of the pomace (grape skins and seeds).

Assemblage/blending: peace, love, and harmony

Several grape varieties are often blended in the barrel or in the tank. This is done when the grapes complement each other particularly well. The result is known as an assemblage or blend. As well as blending different types of grape, you can blend grapes from different plots (sites) or even entire appellations (wine regions), vintages, or barrels. The assemblage happens either before fermentation or before barrel-aging.

To do this, the winemaker uses pipettes to take samples from an array of barrels, puts test blends of about 3 ounces (100 ml) together in various measuring cylinders, and tastes them.

Maturation/aging: yoga class

The wine is now aged (matured) in barrels, tanks, or other fermenters in the cellar. Here it can finally relax and develop—sometimes for up to four years or longer. It can take its time to integrate its tannins, develop its structure, breathe a little, and maybe allow a few aromas from the barrel to also wash over it. In the end, that wine feels silky smooth.

If the winemaker allows it, the wine can now enjoy a few weeks of a treatment known as malolactic fermentation (a secondary fermentation), in which lactic acid bacteria reduce the sharpness of the acidity and makes it milder. This can happen by chance if uncultivated lactic acid bacteria are present, or intentionally by introducing specially cultivated strains of such bacteria into the maturing wine.

Stabilization: a sensitive soul

During its "self-discovery phase," the wine liberates itself from everything negative: Yeast and other particles sink to the bottom of the container.

To guarantee that the wine will maintain its current quality, it can be stabilized (but doesn't have to be). This can prevent tannins, phenols (color), or proteins from forming a film or clouding later on. This stabilization also ensures that the wines remain suitable for cellaring. For this purpose, the wine either has to be moved from one barrel to another, thus removing more and more of the unwanted particles, or fining agents can be added (clay-laden mineral soil, protein-based products), which bind with the particles so that they can be filtered out. The danger here is that certain aromas may also be inadvertently stripped from the wine.

Filtration: Beat it!

Filtration also helps with stabilization. Stubborn yeast particles, bacteria, or proteins need to disappear. White wines and young red wines are often filtered. Long-aged red wines don't need any more filtering, as the particles have already sunk to the bottom with sheer exhaustion.

Filtration methods include the use of large pored cellulose filters or porous membranes that trap the particles, allowing the wine to flow through.

Sulfurization: a stroke of fate

Wine is hypersensitive and hyperactive. The substances in wine can react with anything and everything.

If left to its own devices, wine will continue its journey of self-discovery for a lifetime, continually redefining itself.

Winemakers might have their own ideas, though, and can step in at various stages. They may now add sulfur dioxide, for example, to protect the wine from oxidation and microbiological activity.

Bottling: The time is right!

The wine can be bottled on site or sent to a professional bottler. A third option is renting a mobile bottling machine that actually can be transported from winery to winery.

Depending on the vineyard's philosophy and the style of the wine, the bottles might hit the shelves now, or be allowed to age a little bit more in the bottle; examples of the latter include Rioja *crianza* (one year in bottle), *reserva* (two years in bottle) or *gran reserva* (three years in bottle).

A COMPARISON OF RED WINE AND WHITE WINE PRODUCTION

RED WINE

— Harvest and delivery

— Selection

— Destemming

— Maceration

Two to seven days

Must is repeatedly mixed, so as to extract as many substances as possible. It's up to the winemaker to decide which method to use for mashing.

— Fermentation

Depending on the grape variety and the wine quality, the must can ferment from a few days up to two weeks.

— Pressing

The weight of the grapes in the container causes the fruit to burst. The juice thus separates naturally from the skins (this is the highest quality juice: so-called free-run juice). But the must still contains some juice and a lot of solids. The winemaker can decide whether, and how intensively, to press more juice out of the must.

— Assemblage (blending)

— Maturation/aging (in barrels or tanks)

— Stabilization/filtration

— Bottling

WHITE WINE

— Destemming

— (Possible) Maceration

For only a few hours, if at all. Maceration is less important in white wines because fewer solids (tannins, colors) need to be extracted.

— Pressing

The pressure of the membrane squeezes the juice out of the press basket. Pomace is left behind.

— Fermentation

Depending on the grape variety and the wine quality, the juice can ferment from a few days up to four weeks.

— Assemblage (blending)

— Maturation/aging (in barrels or tanks)

— Stabilization/filtration

— Bottling

RED WINE PRODUCTION

DELIVERY

Harvest time

SELECTION

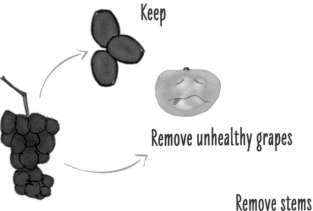

Keep

Remove unhealthy grapes

Remove stems

DESTEMMING

MACERATION

White grape pulp

Red grape skins

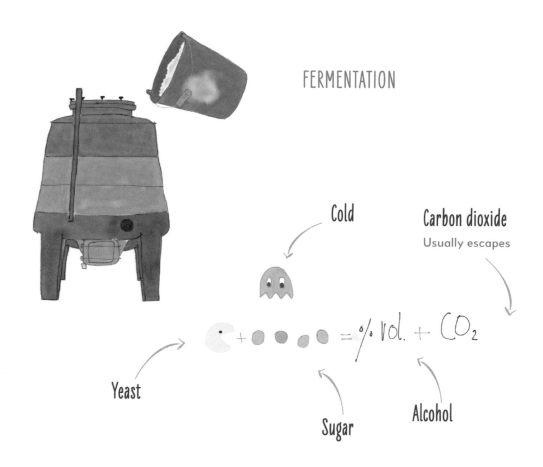

FERMENTATION

Cold

Carbon dioxide
Usually escapes

$$+ \bullet \bullet \bullet \bullet = \% \, vol. + CO_2$$

Yeast

Sugar

Alcohol

PRESSING

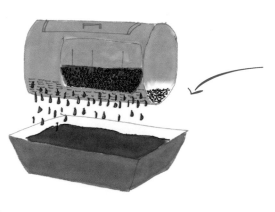

Pneumatic press with balloon
(elastic membrane)

ASSEMBLAGE (BLENDING)

70 percent merlot

30 percent
cabernet sauvignon

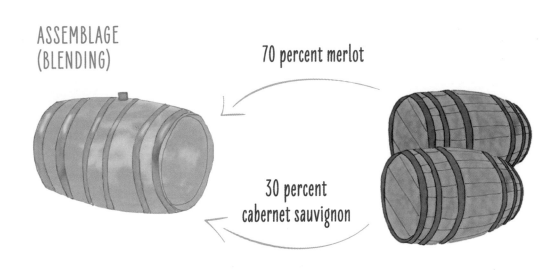

AGING/MATURATION

For wines that gain complexity through
the interaction of oxygen and oak

For fruit-focused wines

FILTRATION

Filtered wine comes out here

Unfiltered wine goes in here

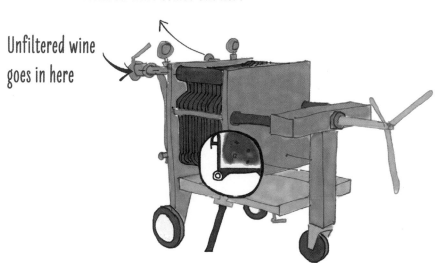

BOTTLING

Château du Edwin.

WHITE WINE PRODUCTION

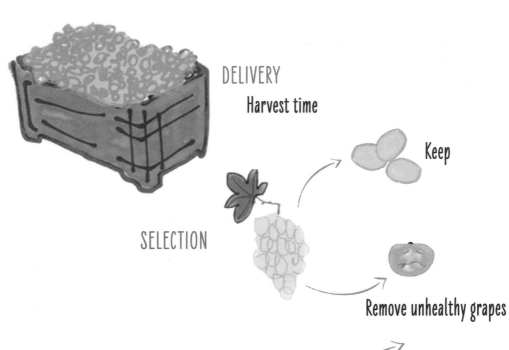

DELIVERY
Harvest time

Keep

SELECTION

Remove unhealthy grapes

DESTEMMING
Remove grape stems

White grape pulp

MACERATION

Yellow grape skin

PRESSING

Pneumatic press with balloon
(elastic membrane)

FERMENTATION

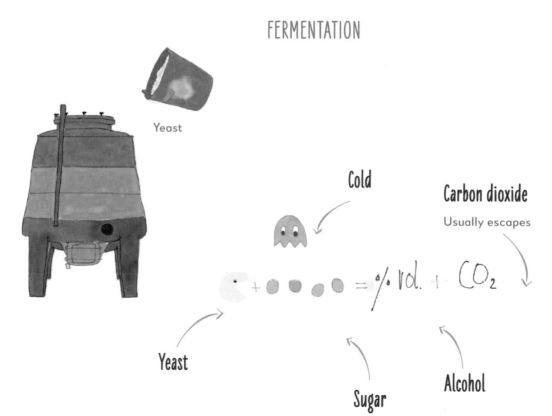

Yeast

Cold

Carbon dioxide

Usually escapes

$$\text{Yeast} + \bullet\bullet\bullet\bullet = \%\ \text{vol.} + CO_2$$

Yeast

Sugar

Alcohol

ASSEMBLAGE (BLENDING)

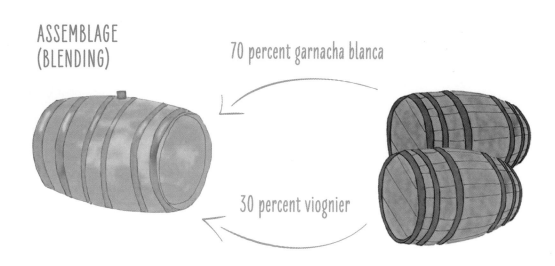

70 percent garnacha blanca

30 percent viognier

AGING/MATURATION

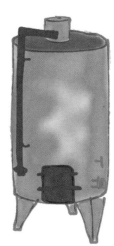

For wines that gain complexity through
the interaction of oxygen and oak

For fruit-focused wines

FILTRATION

Filtered wine comes out here

Unfiltered wine goes in here

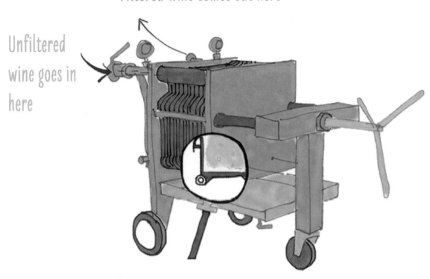

BOTTLING

Domaine de Durst

ROSÉ PRODUCTION

For many people, rosé is the perfect summer drink. Nah, I say rosé's an elixir of life all year round! Fresh, crisp, blush pink, rosé is trending. It's trending more than puppy videos on social media.

But even though people are drinking gallons of the stuff, nobody really knows quite how it's made. Here's how.

Good to know

Blending (assemblage) of white and red wines is not allowed in every wine region; however, it is permitted for making sparkling wine throughout the European Union.

SAIGNÉE

The "infidelity" among production methods
(First one, then the other . . .)

Saignée generally results in dark red, fruity, fuller rosés, made around the world based on the process for red wine.

1. From harvest to destemming, everything is done the same way as the process for making red wine. First, a red wine is made, and from it a rosé is produced on the side.

2. After eight to forty-eight hours of maceration (leaving the must to stand), a hose is used to draw out about 20 percent of the reddish juice from the rest.

3. This extracted, reddish juice is fermented in a separate tank for about ten days.

4. The rest of the juice is made into red wine. As the must of this red wine is now missing 20 percent of the juice, the wine develops a more concentrated structure (skins, seeds, and pulp yield more substance).

5. After the rosé has finished fermenting, the same steps are followed as for making red wine (filtration, etc.). You end up with two wines—a rosé and a red.

DIRECT PRESSING

The "one-night stand" (short process)

Direct pressing generally results in very pale, light rosés, made around the world based on the process for white wine—but with red grapes, of course.

1. From harvest to destemming, everything is done the same way as when making white wine.

2. This is followed by an immediate, yet slower, pressing in stages, until the desired color is reached. This process takes three to four hours. As the juice inevitably also comes into contact with the red skins, the wine does still take on a little more color.

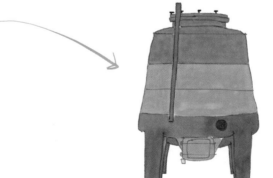

3. The pale pink juice is pumped into a stainless steel tank. Any particles still remaining settle on the bottom.

4. Fermentation and all subsequent stages (filtration, etc.) are carried out the same as for white wine.

SHORT MACERATION

The "affair" (longer process with a foreseeable ending)

Short maceration generally results in pale, lighter rosés, famously made in Provence and Languedoc-Roussillon, based on the process for red and white wine.

1. From harvest to maceration, everything is done the same way as for making red wine. But as when making white wine, the juice comes only briefly into contact with the fruit and seeds.

2. The must is left to stand for six to forty-eight hours, while the juice takes on color and tannins from the skins.

3. The juice is separated from the rest.

4. The juice is drawn off into a stainless steel tank for fermentation.

5. After the rosé has finished fermenting, the same steps are followed as for making white wine (filtration, etc.).

SPARKLING WINE PRODUCTION

BUBBLES

Sparkling wines are wines that froth, tingle, or bubble—i.e., they contain carbon dioxide. They are the most tireless of wines. There are almost as many varieties of sparkling wine as there are wine-producing countries, because these days almost every growing region makes its own "bubbly." Even the Brits, who have a particular love for sparkling wine, have managed to produce respectable bubbly in a rainy country. English sparkling wine is produced using the traditional method with mostly the same grape varieties as Champagne: chardonnay, pinot noir, and pinot meunier, though other grape varieties are allowed. The most famous regions are located in the southeast (Kent, Hampshire, and Surrey).

And North America has options, too! Renowned sparkling wines are produced in Sonoma and the Napa Valley in California with mainly chardonnay, pinot noir, pinot meunier, and pinot blanc grapes. In the Finger Lakes region in New York, rieslings are trending; in Canada, a great up-and-coming wine region is Ontario. And let's not forget about Australia! Their "it" region is Tasmania, where unique sparkling wine is made out of shiraz.

If a sparkling wine has been allowed to bear the name *sekt*, *crémant*, or another term listed below, it must satisfy strict criteria, which vary by region, such as the minimum alcohol content, origin, grape varieties used, minimum maturation period, or a certain pressure inside the bottle.

So, it's particularly important to know where a sparkling wine comes from and how it's made.

And you always thought bubbly was just about fun! Ha!

The two most widely used methods of making sparkling wine are traditional bottle fermentation and tank fermentation.

Good to know

If a sparkling wine has a vintage, this shows that it was a top harvest that year, when only grapes from the year in question were used (base wine). If there isn't a year on the bottle, this is the producer's "calling card wine": a sparkling wine that is intended to taste the same every year, so the base wine is mixed with older vintages. This means the producer can guarantee a consistent quality.

Traditional bottle fermentation (*méthode champenoise, méthode traditionelle, metodo classico*)

The classical way of making sparkling wine is traditional bottle fermentation.

This method is used exclusively for Champagne and premium sparkling wines; it accounts for about 7 percent of sparkling wine made around the world. It is an extremely time-consuming and expensive process, which is reflected in the prices of these top wines.

This is how it's done.

1. Pressing

The grape varieties are carefully pressed separately. Red wine grapes are only pressed briefly so that the skins do not give off too much color or tannin into the white juice. Each sparkling wine region has its own regulations about the number or types of grapes.

Pressing

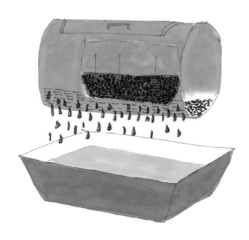

Pinot meunier

Pinot noir

Chardonnay

2. **Fermentation**
   Yeast is added to the grape juice
   (with different grape varieties
   in separate fermenters), which
   turns the sugar into alcohol;
   alternatively, this can be left
   to wild yeasts. The resulting
   carbon dioxide escapes from the
   open vat. This makes the base
   wine, which is separated from
   the yeast.

3. **Assemblage**
   About 70 percent of a
   Champagne consists of the
   base wine from the current
   harvest year. This is mixed
   with older vintages (stored in
   reserve bottles), to guarantee
   that the house style remains
   unchanged over the years. This
   is true of Champagnes without
   a designated vintage year on
   the label. Vintage Champagnes,
   which are only produced in the
   best years, use only the base
   wine from the current harvest.

FIRST FERMENTATION

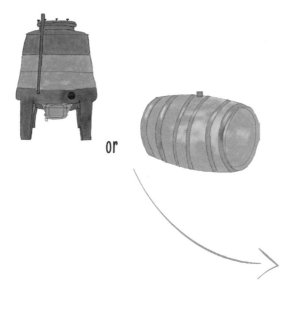

or

ASSEMBLAGE

2015   2011

4. Bottle fermentation

This is key to the sparkle. The blended still wine is bottled and, before being sealed with a crown cap or a natural cork, it's given another little nibble of sugar (sucrose, grape must) and yeast.

The wine now ferments in the bottle for about three weeks. This is what produces our beloved bubbles: During this second fermentation, carbon dioxide forms again, but this time it can't escape from the sealed bottles.

5. Bottle aging

The bottles are stored in the cellar for at least fifteen months. Some producers even leave them to mature on the lees (dead yeast) for over a decade, which can add aromas of freshly baked brioche or apple pie.

BOTTLE FERMENTATION
Second fermentation

Yeast Sugar

BOTTLE AGING

Matures on the lees

6. Riddling

After the sugar has been converted into alcohol and carbon dioxide, the remaining yeast has to be removed from the bottle. The bottles are placed horizontally in a riddling rack, and in the course of twenty-one days, they are slowly and steadily turned, a tenth of a turn per day, and into a vertical position, so that the yeast flows into the neck of the bottle. When large volumes are produced, this work is nowadays done by a robot.

7. Disgorgement

The yeast deposit, now sitting in the neck, is removed by plunging the bottle into a salt-and-ice bath so that it is frozen and ejected when the bottle is opened. The excessive pressure forces the deposit out of the bottle along with a little of the sparkling wine.

8. Dosage

This loss of liquid is made up with wine and cane sugar. The dose of sugar will determine the sweetness of the sparkling wine.

RIDDLING

DOSAGE

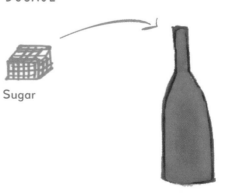

Sugar

9. Corking

Now all that remains is to add the cork and the wire cage. The cage prevents the cork from being pushed out of the bottle by the pressure of the carbon dioxide.

10. Aging

Depending on the criteria in the growing region, the sparkling wine now has to mature in the cellar for a set period. The minimum aging period for German sekt is six months and for Champagne it's fifteen months.

CORKING

AGING

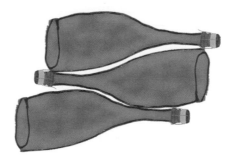

Tank fermentation (*méthode charmat*)

Tank fermentation is a rather less expensive method of producing sparkling wine.

The bubbles are not created in the bottle but under pressure in stainless steel tanks that can hold up to 53,000 gallons (200,000 L). It takes about a year to reach the desired level of carbon dioxide.

This method produces sparkling wines with a less yeasty taste and larger bubbles.

TYPES OF SPARKLING WINE

Here you'll find the most popular sparkling wines in Europe and the US.

Cava

For anyone with expensive taste but without a big budget.

Spanish sparkling wine from the Penedès region, produced like Champagne with traditional bottle fermentation, using macabeo, xarel-lo, and parellada grapes.

Available in the following styles, depending on residual sugar levels:

- Brut Nature (0–3 g/L)
- Extra Brut (0–6 g/L)
- Brut (0–12 g/L)
- Extra Seco (12–17 g/L)
- Seco (17–32 g/L)
- Semiseco (32–50 g/L)
- Dulce (over 50 g/L)

Champagne

For celebrating weddings, births, promotions, signing a contract, buying a house, and other life-changing occasions.

French sparkling wine from the Champagne region, made using traditional bottle fermentation with pinot noir, chardonnay, and pinot meunier grapes.

Available in the following styles, depending on residual sugar levels:

- Brut Nature (non-dosé, zéro dosage) (0–3 g/L)
- Extra Brut (0–6 g/L)
- Brut (0–12 g/L)
- Extra Sec (12–17 g/L)
- Sec (17–32 g/L)
- Demi-Sec (32–50 g/L)
- Doux (over 50 g/L; rare in Champagne)

Crémant

For cultivated parties or as a stylish gift. Ideal for cultured boozing.

Sparkling wines, made using traditional bottle fermentation. Crémants do not come from a single region but can be produced around the world, with well-known examples being Crémant de Loire and Crémant d'Alsace from France, and Crémant de Luxembourg. (For the dosage, see page 124.)

Prosecco

For celebrating the fact that you've survived Monday, Tuesday, or any other day of the week—an Italian sparkling wine from the Veneto and Friuli regions, made using at least 85 percent glera grapes. The remaining 15 percent can be made up of other varieties, such as chardonnay, pinot bianco, pinot grigio, etc.

Prosecco spumante (sparkling)

Quality sparkling wine with at least 3.5 bar carbon dioxide pressure, made using bottle or tank fermentation.

Prosecco frizzante (gently sparkling, slightly fizzy)

Semi-sparkling (*pétillant*) wine with 1 to 2.5 bar carbon dioxide pressure, made from still wine with added carbon dioxide (which is significantly cheaper than the traditional process).

Available in the following styles, depending on residual sugar levels:

- Brut (0–12 g/L)
- Extra Dry (12–17 g/L)
- Dry (17–32 g/L)
- Demi-Sec (32–50 g/L)

Sekt

From Formula One racing to the World Ski Championships, whether first, second, third, or last place: We're celebrating—crack open the sekt!

Quality sparkling wine from German-speaking countries (Germany, Austria), made using traditional bottle fermentation or tank fermentation.

Available in the following styles, depending on residual sugar levels:

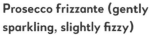

- Naturherb (0–3 g/L)
- Extra Herb (0–6 g/L)
- Herb (0–12 g/L)
- Extra Trocken (12–17 g/L)

SUGAR BAROMETER FOR SPARKLING WINES

SWEET

Residual sugar per liter		French and other sparkling wines	Prosecco	Cava
min. 50 g/L	Sweet	Doux	Demi-Sec	Dulce
32–50 g/L	Medium sweet	Demi-Sec	Demi-Sec	Semiseco
17–32 g/L	Off-dry	Sec	Dry	Seco
12–17 g/L	Dry	Extra Sec	Extra-Dry	Extra Seco
0–12 g/L	Dry	Brut	Brut	Extra Seco
0–6 g/L	Extra dry	Brut	Brut	Brut
0–3 g/L	Bone dry	Brut Nature	Brut	Brut Nature

NOT AT ALL
SWEET,
BONE DRY

EFFECTS ON THE PALATE

PRODUCTION METHODS FOR A SPECIAL MOUTH-FEEL

No kidding: "Mouth-feel" actually is an expression in the wine world. It describes the structure of the wine on your palate. You're sure to have swirled a wine that seemed surprisingly heavy, creamy, and thick (like a maple syrup latte) in your mouth. Or wondered why you could taste vanilla in a red wine, or why a white wine had such an amazing tingle.

Here you'll find a few production methods that are responsible for exactly those effects.

Sur lie: bakery aromas and smoothness

After fermentation, remnants of yeast (lees) linger in the wine. If these aren't filtered out, and the wine continues to mature on the lees (for three or four months, or up to several years), subtle bakery aromas develop, similar to the taste of brioche or croissants. This process is known as *sur lie* (on the lees). It is mainly used for white wines and often for sparkling wines. If the process is carried out in the barrel, it can also give rise to flavors of caramel, cloves, or vanilla, or even a smoky aroma.

Sur lie

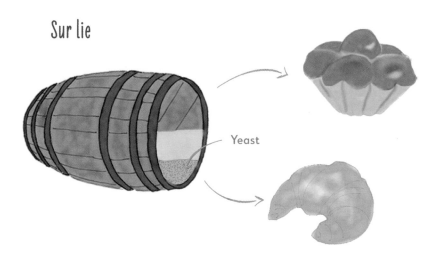

Yeast

BÂTONNAGE

Yeast

Bâtonnage: opulence and volume

During the maturation process, the yeast lees mentioned previously are regularly stirred around with a metal rod (*bâton*) to achieve opulence and a creamier flavor. This process is known as *bâtonnage*, which means "beating up." In wine production, though, it is more of a soft, careful stirring than a fistfight.

Barrel aging: roast aromas

Oak is used in wine aging because it enables the flow of oxygen, which means that the wine can breathe, making it softer, more harmonious, and more complex—rather like us, when we get enough sleep. Red wines benefit particularly from longer barrel aging, as they contain more tannins and color, and these substances integrate into the wine over time. The maturation process varies, according to how much wood comes into contact with the wine.

The larger the barrel, the less contact the wine has with the wood, and consequently, the slower it ages. In a nutshell: Small wooden barrels influence the wine more strongly than large barrels.

The same applies to bottle-aging: In a large bottle (e.g., a magnum: 1.5 L) the wine matures for longer

Good to know

The larger the barrel, the fewer oak flavors and the less oxygen end up in the wine.

ROAST AROMAS

and more slowly than in a 750 ml bottle, as the surface area to total volume ratio is different, though approximately the same amount of oxygen is available in, or able to escape from, both bottles.

But back to the barrels: Oak is useful because the sweetish, spicy tannins from the wood can emphasize the aromas of the wine. Before the bottoms are inserted, the cooper puts the barrel over a fire, which caramelizes the sugars in the wood. The more strongly the wooden barrel is roasted (this is also known in the technical jargon as toasting), the more intense the roast aromas will be: from vanilla to spice notes such as cloves—and from caramel, coffee, and chocolate to charcoal or smoky notes.

Three types of oak are used in aging wine:

- French oak is often used for quality wines because it makes for less obtrusive aromas than other kinds, and gives the wine a velvety, silky structure.

- American oak is very aromatic and is used for more expressive red wines. It produces creamier wines.

- Slovenian oak is used for large wooden barrels and is traditionally used for Italian wines that can mature for decades: Barolo, brunello di Montalcino, Chianti. It has a more neutral aroma.

We distinguish between the following barrel sizes.

* *Barrique* (in Bordeaux): 59 gallons (225 L)

* *Pièce* (mainly in Burgundy): 60 gallons (228 L)

* *Foudre*: 264 to 4,000 gallons (1,000 to 15,000 L)

Effervescence (carbon dioxide)

When a still wine has a slight tingle, it contains a little of the carbon dioxide left over from the fermentation.

During fermentation, the yeast feeds on the fructose (grape sugar) and produces alcohol and carbon dioxide. Before bottling, the carbon dioxide evaporates into the air. But if a wine is bottled before the yeast has finished its work, the interaction between yeast and sugar continues in the closed environment of the bottle. The carbon dioxide is then trapped in the bottle.

Carbon dioxide mainly shows up in still wines if young wines are bottled very quickly. Wines that are aged in wooden barrels for months or years have enough time for the remaining carbon dioxide to disperse in the air before finding its way into the closed world of the bottle.

PHILOSOPHIES OF WINE GROWING

The various philosophies of winemaking are currently one of the hottest topics among wine experts. Animated discussions cover cow patties, sulfur, sheep's skulls, and fish bladders. This often gives rise to the question of whether you can taste the difference between, for example, vegan and organic wine. Question: In a blind test, could you tell the difference between an organic leek and a conventionally grown one? Exactly.

Organic and biodynamic wine growing is not primarily about the taste of the wine, but about the sustainability of the vineyard.

When it comes to natural wines, however, there is a clear difference in taste: These are often unfiltered and unsulfured. They often have aromas and flavors that remind me personally of nuts, overripe oranges, and kombucha. Such oxidative notes are also found in sherries, some of which are matured under a film of yeast known as flor, and are similarly unsulfured. Some people say that this oxidative process blurs or even entirely obliterates the ability to recognize the origins of a natural wine, while others maintain the exact opposite.

Opinion remains just as divided on whether sulfur is the work of the devil and causes headaches and hangovers—or not.

If you ever end up with a glass of natural wine that smells like a farmyard, by the way, leave it to breathe a while. The smell will generally dissipate.

There are, incidentally, a lot of winemakers around the world who work in a highly eco-friendly way but don't have the relevant certification because of the high costs and extra paperwork involved. If need be, this also gives them the option, when faced with a catastrophic natural event, of falling back on tools and resources that can prevent an entire harvest being lost.

Here are the advantages and disadvantages of various winemaking philosophies.

Conventional winemaking
Efficient production methods, the motto being "better safe than sorry."

+ Increased, more reliable harvest yields (sufficient quantities)
+ Moderate production costs
+ Fewer restrictions
− Not very sustainable: Chemical and synthetic crop protection products (herbicides, fungicides, pesticides) are allowed.
− Use of technology to improve wine
− The use of flavor enhancers, such as wood chips

Controlled, integrated winemaking
Nature-based production methods, the motto being "less is more."

+ Protection for people: Crop protection products are gentle on the environment and benefit insects. Stricter guidelines for spraying and fertilizer use requires certification.
− Use of technology to improve wine
− The use of flavor enhancers, such as citric acid

VEGAN

Vegan winemaking

No animals in the grapes please!

+ Wine is in and of itself a
  vegetarian product, but animal
  products are often used in
  fining and clarifying, so that
  the wine doesn't go cloudy
  (egg white, milk proteins,
  gelatin, fish bladders). Vegan
  wine production avoids these
  additives and uses herbal
  products such as clay minerals
  or pea protein instead. The
  finished wine contains,
  at most, minute traces of
  clarifying agents, which
  cannot be tasted.
− It's a bureaucratic marathon to
  receive official certification.

Natural winemaking

Stark-naked minimalism.

+ Based on organic or
  biodynamic growing methods
+ As little intervention as
  possible during winemaking
  (no additives)
+ Only wild yeast used in
  fermentation, no cultured
  yeast
+ Nothing extracted from the
  wine, either by filtration or by
  fining
− Not defined under wine law
  (so no recognized inspection
  body)
− Cellaring/aging potential not
  always guaranteed: The wine
  can change from one day to the
  next.

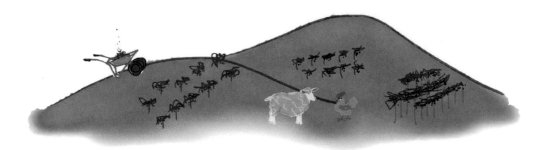

Organic winemaking

Holistic production methods "in the name of Mother Nature."

+ Prioritizes a healthy ecosystem
+ Promotes biodiversity
+ Only natural fertilizers; disease control without chemical, synthetic products
+ Strict certification guidelines
− More expensive, more labor-intensive, more strenuous
− Higher risk of crop failure because of the more limited options for intervention compared to conventional wine growing

Organic-biodynamic winemaking

Closed cycle, the motto being "three cheers for homeopathy."

+ Organic wine growing a precondition
+ Work in the vineyards and cellars according to the lunar calendar
+ Exclusively natural resources: nine preparations (e.g., compost)
+ Promotes biodiversity, ensures a natural balance, and promotes the vine's immune system
− More expensive, more labor-intensive, more strenuous
− Higher risk of a crop failure because of the more limited options for intervention compared to conventional wine growing

The key to biodynamics lies in seeing winemaking as a living system in its entirety. To this end, the biodynamic vineyards should be closed, self-maintaining systems. Biodynamics regards the winery or the vineyard in the context of lunar and cosmic rhythms.

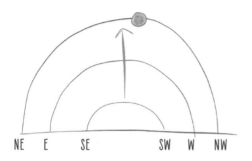

NE E SE SW W NW

The waxing moon

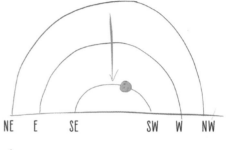

NE E SE SW W NW

The waning moon

We can't underestimate the power of the moon, given that it causes the tides to ebb and flow.

Here are some of the key principles of biodynamic agriculture.

While the moon is rising (the moon's arc is slightly higher every day), sap levels increase strongly in plants. Energy is focused on what's happening above the ground.

The following work is done:

• Spray horn silica (see page 134) on the fields

• Harvesting

• Sowing seeds.

While the moon is descending (the moon's arc is slightly lower every day), the energy is focused underground. The following work is done:

• Pruning vines

• Planting in dormant plots

• Making and distributing compost

• Cultivating vines

• Spray cow horn manure (see page 134) on the fields.

From the holistic view taken in biodynamic cultivation, the ground is seen not just as a carrier for plant growth but as an organism in its own right. There is also a series of special preparations to be used to improve the soil quality, applied at certain times in harmony with the rhythms of nature. Diseases or problems in the field or vineyard are not fought individually but seen as a problem within the cycle as a whole. Correct the problem in the system and the problem will solve itself.

The following biodynamic preparations serve as sprays or compost for the fields.

500   **Cow horn manure**
Cow horns are filled with cow manure and buried in the ground; the contents are later thinned with water and sprayed over the fields.
→ Acts like fertilizer: stimulates soil activity and root growth.

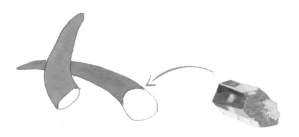

502

Yarrow
Yarrow flowers are fermented in a stag's bladder, which is then hung to dry and buried in the ground before it is used as fertilizer.
→ Improves the availability of minerals for the plant.

501

Horn silica
Cow horns are filled with ground quartz and buried in the ground; the contents are later thinned with water and sprayed over the fields.
→ Promotes plant metabolism and strengthens their immune system against pests.

503

Chamomile

Chamomile flowers are stuffed into dried-out cow's intestines.

➡ Promotes nitrogen in fertilizer.

504

Stinging nettle

Stinging nettles are packed in dirt, then added to compost or liquid manure.

➡ Strengthens weak or less vital vines.

505 Oak bark

Oak bark is fermented in an animal skull.

➡ Protects against fungal pathogens and acts as an insecticide.

506

Dandelion

Dandelion is fermented in dried-out cow's intestines.

➡ Promotes the nutrient supply to the vines.

507

Valerian

A solution of valerian flowers is added to the compost.

➡ Promotes the formation of flowers and fruit on the vines.

508

Horsetail preparation

Dried horsetail is mixed with rainwater and sprayed over the vines.

➡ Protects against fungal attacks, rot, and mildew.

SULFUR
The preservative for wine

Since the issue of sulfur is a big one right now, let's take a brief digression here. Sulfur ensures the shelf life and characteristic aromas of wines. Think of dried apple rings: Unsulfured ones are brown while sulfured ones stay white. And it's just the same with wine. Sulfur protects against oxidation and also keeps the flavors and aromas in the wine from undesirable changes.

Everything you need to know about sulfur

- Sulfur dioxide (SO_2) is added to wine, not pure sulfur.

- Sulfites are salts of sulfurous acid, but the term is used as a synonym for sulfur dioxide.

- In conventional winemaking, sulfur dioxide can be added to the wine during maceration and after fermentation, fining, filtration, and/or bottling.

- Sulfite levels of more than 10 mg/L must be declared on the bottle.

- Sulfites are not generally responsible for a headache the next day. If you feel that you react badly to sulfites, try eating a packet of dried fruit to test whether you're allergic. They can contain over 2,000 mg of sulfur dioxide per kilogram.

- Sugar and tannins have an equally preservative effect. The more residual sugar or tannins there are in the wine, the less sulfur dioxide it needs.

- Despite all the advantages of sulfur dioxide, many winemakers are striving to do without additives—the less added or subtracted from the wine, the better and healthier.

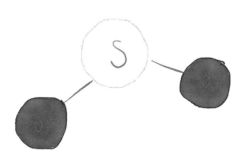

PERMITTED SULFUR CONTENT IN RELATION TO RESIDUAL SUGAR

	WHITE/ROSÉ WINES	RED WINES
Conventional	200 mg/L SO₂ for up to 5 g/l residual sugar 250 mg/L SO₂ from 5 g/L residual sugar or more	150 mg/L SO₂ for up to 5 g/L residual sugar 200 mg/L SO₂ from 5 g/L residual sugar or more
Controlled, integrated	200 mg/L SO₂ for up to 5 g/L residual sugar 250 mg/L SO₂ from 5 g/L residual sugar or more	150 mg/L SO₂ for up to 5 g/L residual sugar 200 mg/L SO₂ from 5 g/L residual sugar or more
Organic	150 mg/L SO₂ for up to 2 g/L residual sugar 170 mg/L SO₂ for 2–5g/L residual sugar 220 mg/L SO₂ from 5 g/L residual sugar or more	100 mg/L SO₂ for up to 2 g/L residual sugar 120 mg/L SO₂ for 2–5 g/L residual sugar 170 mg/L SO₂ from 5 g/L residual sugar or more
Organic-biodynamic	150 mg/L SO₂ for up to 2 g/L residual sugar 170 mg/L SO₂ for 2–5 g/L residual sugar 220 mg/L SO₂ from 5 g/L residual sugar or more	100 mg/L SO₂ for up to 2 g/L residual sugar 120 mg/L SO₂ for 2–5 g/L residual sugar 170 mg/L SO₂ from 5 g/L residual sugar or more
Natural wine	Generally no added sulfur. No guidelines. Some winemakers recommend 30 mg/L SO₂ (can even occur naturally).	
Vegan wine	Uses no animal-based additives but is not necessarily organic. Must keep at least to the minimum guidelines for conventional wine. If certified as organic or biodynamic, the relevant wine laws must be adhered to.	

Appendix

GLOSSARY

This glossary is not intended to be either complete or unmanageably extensive—it is just a means to an end. If you're familiar with the terms here, there's nothing to hold you back from standing tall, glass in hand (held by the stem of course!), and talking wine with the best of them. And that's really what it's all about.

amarone: red wine from Valpolicella in the Veneto region, made partly using dried and consequently highly concentrated grapes.

Barbaresco: red wine from nebbiolo grapes, from Barbaresco, Piedmont (Italy).

Barolo: red wine from nebbiolo grapes from Barolo, Piedmont.

barrique: wooden barrel that can hold 59 gallons (225 L) of wine. Wines are often aged in barriques to make them smoother, and/or so that they'll take on woody aromas.

blend: different grape varieties blended together to produce a more complex, well-balanced wine than one made with just a single variety.

bouquet: the smell of a wine in the glass (e.g., a floral or fruity bouquet).

Brix scale (°Bx): measures the density of the must (mostly sugar) in the grape on the vine. The must weight can be used to assess the alcohol content of the future wine (for instance, 24°Bx means 14.4 percent alcohol). The Brix scale also plays a role in determining the time of the harvest.

brunello: red wine from sangiovese grapes from the village of Montalcino, Tuscany.

Chablis: wine made from chardonnay grapes from Chablis, Burgundy (France).

Châteauneuf-du-Pape: white or red wine from the village of that name in the southern Rhône Valley. Red wines mainly from grenache, syrah, and mourvèdre grapes. White wines made from the grenache blanc, clairette blanche, piquepoul blanc, and bourboulenc grape varieties.

Chianti: red wine primarily from sangiovese from the Chianti region in Tuscany.

closed: description of a wine that doesn't exude any aromas (you might want to start swirling your glass or decant the wine).

complex: description of a wine with a certain density and multilayeredness (whatever that means!).

concentrated: generally positive description of a wine with complexity and depth. A substantial, complex wine, which might need to breathe a while before you can enjoy it.

cru: in France this denotes a site that is generally better rated than other locations based on terroir, and can thus deliver better wines. Some of these crus were designated "champions" hundreds of years ago, however, so a little skepticism may be warranted.

cuvée: in Champagne, the first pressed (and best quality) juice. More often the word is used to describe a blend that is made of multiple grape varieties from different barrels or vats.

extraction: a process mainly used in making red wine. During maceration and fermentation, solids (colors, tannins) are extracted from the grape skins.

fermentation: the process in which yeast turns sugar into alcohol.

flat: description of a wine that lacks acidity. It's "dull" like water.

harmonious: description of a well-balanced wine without obtrusive aromas.

indigenous: native vine varieties that have their origin in the place where they grow. They only thrive in their original home. If you transplant them to another region, there is a danger that they'll die or not reach their full potential. Examples include Roero arneis (Italy), zinfandel (USA), and touriga nacional (Portugal).

kabinett: quality label for wines that meet a series of very different conditions, depending on the country and region. Roughly speaking, in Germany it is a category of quality wine (Prädikatswein), and in Austria it means a wine that has to fulfill strict legal criteria.

malolactic fermentation: this usually takes place after the alcoholic fermentation. Lactic acid bacteria reduce the harsh sharpness of the acidity and make it milder so that the wine tastes softer.

must: gooey mixture of fruit pulp, seeds, skins, and juice.

pomace: or *marc*. The solid remains of grapes (or other fruit) after pressing—skin, pulp, seeds, and stems.

Pouilly-Fuissé: white wine from chardonnay grapes in the Pouilly-Fuissé region, Burgundy.

Pouilly-Fumé: white wine from sauvignon blanc grapes from the Pouilly-Fumé region, Loire.

Prädikatswein: the highest quality rating for German wines. They can range from dry to ultra-sweet.

reserve: general term for a wine that enjoyed a longer aging in the barrel and/or in the bottle.

ripasso: full-bodied red wine from the Veneto region combined with pomace from amarone production.

ripe: description of a wine with aromas of dried fruits such as figs or plums. Overly ripe notes can make a wine reminiscent of jam.

Sancerre: white wine from sauvignon slanc grapes from the village of Sancerre, Loire.

sediment: also called deposit. Over the years, solids (tannins and leftover particles from the grape skins) separate from the wine and settle at the bottom of the bottle. It won't kill anyone and doesn't affect the quality in any way.

sparkling wines: wines, such as sekt and Champagne, which contain carbon dioxide.

still wines: white, rosé, and red wines with no carbon dioxide—just ordinary wine.

tannins: naturally occurring compounds from grape skins, seeds, and stems, which can have a drying effect on the mouth. Mainly found in red wines.

NAMES OF WINES

White wine

chardonnay (worldwide)

chasselas (Vaud, Switzerland) = fendant (Valais, Switzerland) =
gutedel (Germany)

muscat (France) = moscato (Italy)

pinot blanc (France) = pinot bianco (Italy, Spain) =
weißburgunder (Germany, Switzerland) = Klevner (Austria)

pinot grigio (Italy) = pinot gris (France) = grauburgunder (Germany)

Red wine

carignan (France) = cariñena (Spain) = carignano (Italy)

grenache (France) = garnacha (Spain) = cannonau (Italy)

pinot noir (worldwide) = pinot nero (Italy) =
blauburgunder (Switzerland) = spätburgunder (Germany)

syrah (worldwide) = shiraz (Australia)

zinfandel (USA) = primitivo (Italy)

INDEX

cellaring, wines for, 22–23

Chablis, 140

chamomile, 135

Champagne, 122

chardonnay, 23, 68, 117

chasselas, 68

Châteauneuf-du-Pape, 140

cheese and wine pairing, 16

chenin blanc, 70

Chianti, 140

church windows, 28–29

climate, 45, 52, 54–55

closed wine, 140

closures, 10–11

clouds, 55

complex wine, 140

concentrated wine, 140

controlled, integrated winemaking, 130, 137

conventional winemaking, 130, 137

corks, 10–11, 121

cork taint, 32–33

cow horn manure, 134

crémant, 123

crus, 140

cuvée, 140

D

dandelion, 135

dates, 18

decanting wine, 8–9

destemming, 99

dinner, 20

disgorgement, 120

dosage, 120

Douro/Duero River region, 86

E

extraction, 140

F

family gatherings, 19

fermentation
 aromas and, 46
 defined, 141
 malolactic, 100, 141
 sparkling wine, 117–21
 still wine, 99, 103, 105, 109
 tank, 121
 traditional bottle, 117–21

filtration, 101, 107, 111

finish, 48

flat wine, 141

flaws, wine, 32–33

food and wine pairing, 13–16

France, 78–80

French oak, 126

G

gamay, 72

garnacha blanca, 69

Germany, 89

gewürztraminer, 70

gifts, 17

glasses, wine, 2–3, 6

glossary, 140–41

grape varieties, 68–76

grauburgunder, 69

grenache, 72

grüner veltliner, 23, 69

gutedel, 68

R

red grape varieties, 72–76
red wine
  glasses, 2
  names, 142
  production, 103–7
  serving temperature, 4, 5
  shelf life, 7
  styles, 41
  sulfur content, 137
regions, wine, 77–95
reserve, 141
riddling, 120
riesling, 23, 71
ripasso, 141
ripe wine, 141
roast aromas, 126–28
rosé, 4, 5, 7, 112–15, 137

S

saignée, 113
Sancerre, 141
sangiovese, 75
sauvignon blanc, 17, 70
sayings, impressive, 31, 49
screw caps, 10–11
secondary aromas, 45–46
sediment, 141
sekt, 123
serving temperature, 4–5
shelf life, 7
shiraz, 76
Slovenian oak, 126
soil, 52, 58–63
Spain, 84, 86
sparkling wine
  defined, 141

glasses, 3
production, 116–21
serving temperature, 4, 5
shelf life, 7
sugar barometer, 124
types, 122–23
vintage versus calling card, 116
stabilization, 101
stains, wine, 21
still wine, 98–102, 141
  See also red wine; rosé; white wine
stinging nettle, 135
styles, wine, 38–41
sugar, 35–36, 124
sulfur, 32–33, 136–37
sulfurization, 102
sun, 54
sur lie, 125
sweet wines, 37
Switzerland, 87
syrah, 76

T

tank fermentation, 121
tannins, 35, 141
tasting
  appearance, 28–29
  aroma, 30–31
  aroma cross, 42–43
  aroma development, 44–47
  flaws, wine, 32–33
  overall impression, 48–49
  palate, 34–35
  styles/characters, wine, 38–41
tempranillo, 19, 73
terrain, 52, 56–57
terroir
  climate, 52, 54–55
  soil, 52, 58–63

ACKNOWLEDGMENTS

To my family: Thank you for your patience and endless enthusiasm. I love every moment I can spend doing everything wine with you.

And to all the wine women who opened every door for me, so that I can stand here today with my own book.

ABOUT THE AUTHOR

MADELYNE MEYER is the marketing manager for the Wine Cellars of Aarau—her family's business for five generations. A certified wine specialist, she studied at the INSEEC Wine and Spirits Institute in Bordeaux. She lives in Switzerland.

The Experiment, LLC
220 East 23rd Street, Suite 600
New York, NY 10010-4658
theexperimentpublishing.com

THE EXPERIMENT and its colophon are registered trademarks of The Experiment, LLC. Many of the designations used by manufacturers and sellers to distinguish their products are claimed as trademarks. Where those designations appear in this book and The Experiment was aware of a trademark claim, the designations have been capitalized.

The Experiment's books are available at special discounts when purchased in bulk for premiums and sales promotions as well as for fund-raising or educational use. For details, contact us at info@theexperimentpublishing.com.

Library of Congress Cataloging-in-Publication Data

Names: Meyer, Madelyne, author.
Title: Welcome to wine : an illustrated guide to all you really need to
   know / written and illustrated by Madelyne Meyer.
Description: New York : The Experiment, 2020. | Includes index.
Identifiers: LCCN 2020026943 (print) | LCCN 2020026944 (ebook) | ISBN
   9781615197026 | ISBN 9781615197033 (ebook)
Subjects: LCSH: Wine and wine making.
Classification: LCC TP548 .M53 2020 (print) | LCC TP548 (ebook) | DDC
   641.2/2--dc23
LC record available at https://lccn.loc.gov/2020026943
LC ebook record available at https://lccn.loc.gov/2020026944

ISBN 978-1-61519-702-6
Ebook ISBN 978-1-61519-703-3

Cover design by Beth Bugler
Text design by AT Verlag
Illustrations by Madelyne Meyer
Illustrations on pages 61 and 62 recreated from original illustrations in *Stein und Wein* by
   Kündig Rainer (AS Verlag, 2018)
Author photograph by WASERHEPP

Manufactured in China

First printing October 2020
10 9 8 7 6 5 4 3 2 1